ENACTing Change

ENACTing Change

A Handbook for Teaching Advocacy and Civic Engagement

KATHLEEN COLE, ROBERT W. GLOVER,

RICHARD J. MEAGHER, and KATHARINE A. OWENS

Edited by Melissa Stimell

BRANDEIS UNIVERSITY PRESS

Waltham, Massachusetts

Brandeis University Press

Manufactured in the United States of America

LIBRARY OF CONGRESS CATALOGING-IN-PUBLICATION DATA
available at https://catalog.loc.gov/
cloth ISBN # 978-1-68458-291-4
paper ISBN # 978-1-68458-283-9
e-book ISBN # 978-1-68458-284-6

5 4 3 2 1

Contents

Editor's Preface vii

Introduction 1

1 Teaching an ENACT Course 15

2 Building Relationships at Your State Legislature 41

3 Legislative Research 59

4 Meeting with Legislators 93

5 Engaging with the Public 127

6 Life after ENACT 147

Conclusion 163

Acknowledgments 173
Bibliography 175
Contributors 179
Index 181

Editor's Preface

In the spring semester of the 2009–10 academic year, I embarked on an experiment with thirteen dedicated Brandeis University undergraduate students and the logistical, financial, and intellectual support of the Brandeis University International Center for Ethics, Justice and Public Life and the Legal Studies Program. Together we created "Advocacy for Policy Change."

"Advocacy for Policy Change" is dedicated to the creation of informed citizens: individuals prepared and motivated to be active citizens in our democracy. This course combines an investigation of the ethical dilemmas that arise in the process of lawmaking with hands-on engagement at the state level. Students are encouraged to think deeply about the complexities of shaping laws for constituents who hold diverse viewpoints and how best to progress through the legislative process.

"Advocacy for Policy Change" became the catalyst for ENACT: The Abraham Feinberg Educational Network for Active Civic Transformation, a national, nonpartisan, intercollegiate program based at Brandeis University. My Brandeis colleagues and I support ENACT faculty fellows as they develop and teach their own ENACT experiential courses at colleges and universities across the United States. ENACT has become a major voice in addressing challenges to American democracy by engaging young people around the country in civic discourse and activism built on knowledge, cooperation, justice, and integrity.

In ENACT courses, students work in teams to design and implement models of legislative engagement. State legislators and organizations advise each team to help them understand the lawmaking process, connect with colleagues, and set realistic goals. Each student completes a series of assignments related to the project, in formats relevant to the legislative process, such as a legislative research report, an elevator speech, and an op-ed.

Students learn how to work with state legislators, legislative staff members, and community organizations to advance policy. With assistant directors David Weinstein and Charlotte Powley, we have developed a robust national network of faculty, students, and alumni that includes an online platform for resource sharing and ongoing assessment. ENACT supports meaningful collaboration across our universities, which include public and private institutions, four-year and two-year colleges, a military academy, historically Black colleges, Hispanic-serving institutions, and a tribal college.

ENACT's development was supported by a generous multiyear commitment from Brandeis University International Center for Ethics, Justice and Public Life board member Norbert Weissberg and his wife, Judith Schneider. ENACT's continued expansion has been supported by a multiyear grant from the Teagle Foundation's "Education for American Civic Life" initiative, which enabled ENACT to expand across the country.

I must thank several people whose support has been critical to ENACT's success. ENACT would not exist without the support of Brandeis University professor emeritus Richard Gaskins, my mentor and the former director of the legal studies program. He and Daniel Terris, director emeritus of the International Center for Ethics, Justice and Public Life, took the kernel of a unique idea and made it a reality. Former Massachusetts state representative Jay Kaufman, Brandeis '68, MA '73, helped me create a course worthy of Brandeis University. Massachusetts state senator Becca Rausch, Brandeis '01, and her staff have been invaluable: hosting us at the State House, speaking to the class, and making introductions to her fellow legislators. An exceptional group of teaching assistants has ensured that the course runs smoothly each year.

I am most thankful to the authors for joining me in this experiment, adapting the ENACT model to fit the needs of their students and institutions, and sharing it beyond our immediate ENACT network. We look forward to supporting the next cohort of ENACT informed citizens and the continued growth of ENACT.

MELISSA STIMELL
Director, ENACT: The Abraham Feinberg Educational Network for Active Civic Transformation
Professor of the Practice in Legal Studies
Brandeis University

ENACTing Change

Introduction

Three college baseball players—two juniors and a first-year student they had taken under their wing—decided to sign up for an unusual course they had seen promoted the previous spring. Offered during the specialized January term on their small liberal arts campus, the course promised to help "examine how citizens can change state policy." But what really caught their eye was this sentence: "Students will identify a bill currently active in the state legislature and develop and execute a step-by-step plan for helping to get it enacted or defeated." Passing a bill? A real one? As college students?

It turned out the class, Politics in Action, did not exactly *require* them to pass a bill. But as they quickly found out, they were certainly required to try. The experience turned out to be a four-week crash course in policy advocacy, immersing them in the legislative process in their state. They spent a day learning how the state legislature works, then went immediately to the legislature, wandering around the offices and visiting the capitol building. They were introduced to the state legislative database, an online browser that returned hundreds of results for keywords like "education" and "firearms." They were asked to identify a bill they liked and come up with some information, ideas, and materials about why to make it a law. And then, they were set loose upon the world, released into the legislative offices to try to get legislators to vote for their bill.

These three students found that they loved this challenge. They found a bill that increased funding for high school counselors, something that at least one of them knew a bit about due to a friend's struggles with mental health. They not only developed a factsheet full of arguments and data to leave behind with legislators but also created a "consulting firm" for themselves, with a logo that they plastered all over their documents. They ended up meeting the bill's sponsor, who was so excited and supportive of their advocacy that they joked that the legislator had "adopted" them for the session.

After all that, the bill did *not* pass, left in committee due to an anticipated lack of money in the budget. But by the time the class was over, the students had been repeatedly told that passage, while welcome, was largely beside the point, at least for the short term. In a reflection paper they submitted at the end of the four-week term, these students seemed undaunted and hopeful. "Regardless of income, status, or age," they wrote, "policy advocates can be effective in creating change at the state level if they are dedicated enough." Their most surprising lesson from their time at the state legislature? They watched a state representative tell a staffer to push off a meeting with another state official just so he could hear more of what the students had to say about school counselors. "They really do care about what we have to say," they wrote.

The two juniors finished their successful undergraduate careers, went on to law school as planned, and were hired into law firms. Their first-year protégé, however, seemed a bit more affected by his advocacy experience. He ended up interning for a state legislative office, then joined another legislator's campaign for higher office. After his candidate was successfully elected, the student joined up after graduation as a special assistant and liaison to the legislature. Later he would say, "I wouldn't be here" if it weren't for that advocacy course.

Stories like this are playing out in college courses all across the nation. The Politics in Action course these students completed is part of a national program called ENACT, a model advocacy course developed at Brandeis University and offered in and around state capitals. The course enables college teachers to get students excited about politics, about legislative advocacy, and about making the world a better place. The point of this book is to show you that you can do it too.

Civic Crisis

Experts widely agree: there is a crisis in civic education. Roughly twenty years ago, astute observers cautioned that "levels of political knowledge, engagement, and political enthusiasm are so low as to threaten the vitality and stability of democratic politics in the United States."[1]

The ensuing years have seen a measurable erosion of the foundational knowledge, attitudes, and methods of engagement that undergird a stable democracy. It is easy to observe a number of effects: the absence of basic political literacy,[2] the contagion of political misinformation,[3] and the seeming ease with which self-interested actors weaponize latent societal distrust for political gain.[4] As a result, our democratic institutions have, both metaphorically and literally, come under attack.

Still, all may not be lost. While youth seem to drive the declines and rejection in political and civic engagement, many young people also seem to recognize the dearth of meaningful engagement in civic life. Many seek out opportunities, both within and without institutions of higher education, to take on civically oriented projects and problem-solving. Educators across a number of disciplines continue to note how students eye education, and particularly a college degree, as not just a means to gainful employment but also as a way to live meaningful lives. As a result, a number of instructors have incorporated purposeful and consequential activities that directly engage students in political action.

Indeed, the past decade has provided numerous examples of the ways that empowered students can engage in transformative political action: on climate change,[5] within the movement to end gun violence,[6] and working to condemn violence by law enforcement and support the Black Lives Matter movement.[7] Similarly, student interest in service learning, volunteerism, and engagement with public issues has ticked up.[8] At the same time, educators across the country are reinvigorating civic education, offering ambitious proposals befitting the urgency and scope of our contemporary crisis.[9]

This book comes from this latter perspective: a place of hope in the future of our citizenry. In many ways, this book is about empowerment—both empowering educators who want to bring exciting and impactful opportunities to their students and empowering students to effect legislative change. While we recognize the steep challenges that face political decision makers in our country, we strongly believe that education can be a force not just for background information and basic skills but also for preparing people for active citizenry. The model course we present in this book is not just about pedagogy, but also about citizenship.

About ENACT

ENACT: The Abraham Feinberg Educational Network for Active Civic Transformation is a collaborative higher education initiative developed at Brandeis University in 2016. In subsequent years, ENACT has expanded to support faculty across the United States in creating undergraduate courses focused on developing state-level policy advocacy skills, directly seeking to engage "young people around the country in civic activism built on knowledge, cooperation, justice, and integrity."[10] ENACT identifies a faculty fellow in each state who commits to developing a recurring course at their home institution based on the ENACT model. Each ENACT course is carefully designed to align with the unique characteristics of the educational institution in which it is embedded, the needs of students, and the political culture of the state in which it is offered.

What unites ENACT courses happening across the United States is a shared mission centered on core learning outcomes. While ENACT instructors are interested in political engagement, they do not forget to emphasize *knowledge*. Students in these courses should "develop critical awareness of the gap between the actual legislative process and theoretical or popular descriptions; distinguish legislative perspectives from related concerns; [and] identify the complex roles of the citizen advocate." ENACT offerings also entail an emphasis on practical *skills*: students "increase oral and written facility in expressing arguments under political constraints; synthesize and evaluate information from diverse sources representing competing philosophies; [and] create models of solving challenging problems of social justice through legislative means." Lastly, and perhaps most importantly, ENACT courses are united in their focus on students' enlarged understanding and appreciation of *justice*: they should "grasp the challenges of achieving justice through legislation; test one's own justice commitments against current state and national problems; compare justice arguments over time; [and] contribute to the creation of a just society through legislative means."[11]

As a result, ENACT courses ensure that the advocacy in which students are engaged involves real consequences. Students identify and advocate for actual bills pending before actual legislators, which raises the stakes for the students as individuals and as community members. Such work not only builds knowledge and skills but also enhances that knowledge by engaging students in the development of important skills of communication, persuasion, argument, critical thinking, and strategy.

As ENACT faculty fellows and participants in the ENACT network, the authors of this volume have helped develop and implement the ENACT model in their own courses, institutions, and states. ENACT continues to provide intensive support for its designated fellows, and leaders within the network seek to promote this transformative approach with a wider audience. With this volume, the authors hope to share this innovative model with educators across the country and invite them to partake in this transformative work.

> *This class was my first opportunity to directly engage with the government and to fully dedicate my ideas into policy changes.*
>
> —response from ENACT survey, Brandeis University

The ENACT Course Model

As we will argue throughout this book, the ENACT course model is adaptable to a variety of contexts and circumstances. Still, the model is built out of a handful of core components pulled from the original Brandeis course, with each identified below.

ENACT instructors often start the class with an overview of state government and their legislature. ENACT does not require the depth of knowledge often provided by a standard undergraduate state government class, although the model has been incorporated into such classes. Still, even advanced political science majors may need some basic instruction in state institutions and contextual knowledge about your particular state's legislative processes. Lectures, discussions, and other activities in the early part of your class can draw on introductory readings from a state and local government textbook, as well as stories from local news outlets or resources provided by your state legislature.

The heart of the course involves engaging students in legislative advocacy. ENACT emphasizes collaboration, and so instructors are next encouraged to guide students through working in pairs or groups to identify a bill and advocate for its passage. Models for group work vary widely, and ENACT has proven a fit for many of these; while we offer suggestions below, instructor experience is probably the most important guide to the specific structure of collaboration in your course.

Students can complete a variety of assignments during their advocacy work, but typical tasks include research reports and presentations on their chosen advocacy issue and/or bill; the development of advocacy materials, including "one-pagers" and letters to legislators; production of social media posts and multimedia campaigns; and more traditional civic engagement assignments, such as letters to the editor. At various points in the advocacy process, students and instructors may find it helpful to engage with existing advocacy groups and coalitions for guidance and information about their chosen bill. Many pedagogical models emphasize the importance of culminating assignments, particularly those that incorporate reflection, in helping students synthesize knowledge and prepare for future action. The ENACT model is no different, and we offer below a few different suggestions for putting a "capstone" on the ENACT experience. (Detailed guidelines and suggestions for these assignments and activities are included in later chapters.)

The core student experience of the ENACT model is advocacy meetings with legislators, preferably in context at legislative offices and/or committee hearings. We encourage instructors to build courses around these experiences, at least as much as logistics permit. Still, even without this core component, it is possible to incorporate other elements of the ENACT model into a variety of courses. No matter how much ENACT you are able to use in your particular campus context, we believe the model's elements can still prepare your students for a more active role in future citizenship.

> *It was the first time I had ever visited a statehouse, lobbied public officials. It demystified the whole process. I now feel confident reaching out to public officials. I feel like I know how to frame issues in terms of values.*
>
> —from a survey of Brandeis alumni who participated in ENACT course

Why ENACT?

So why should an educator interested in achieving these outcomes use the ENACT framework as a means to do so? Perhaps most centrally, the ENACT model was conceived with *active, experiential learning* at its core. There are many ways to potentially achieve the outcomes mentioned above, but in this case the outcomes and the means of achieving them have been carefully crafted alongside one another. Students in ENACT courses are challenged to engage directly in policy research, political advocacy, and strategic communications in settings where the issues are tangible and the stakes are real. This is an exhilarating experience for educators and students alike.

ENACT focuses energy on the *state* level of political decision-making, an often overlooked arena of political engagement and impact. The scale of politics at the national level can make it much more difficult to see change; engaging with national issues in our current polarized, gridlocked political environment may even lead to students feeling disempowered and disconnected from policymaking. By contrast, most state legislatures are still relatively localized and accessible bodies, with staffers and even elected officials still responsive to their constituents. On this smaller and more community-oriented scale, it is often possible to know and become known, to gain policy expertise, and to make an impact on a bill's passage. States also are in many ways "where the action is" in terms of policymaking, with dramatically increased capacity and responsibility over the past few decades.

The ENACT model is *evidence-based*, generating impressive results in helping students achieve the learning outcomes laid out above. Published research from the course already shows an increased sense of political efficacy and effectiveness from students.[12] And the ENACT program is actively engaging in longer-term analysis of the lasting impacts that the program has on its program alumni long after participation in the course, often overlooked in existing research on the impacts of engaged, experiential pedagogies. (We will discuss this evidence more in the Conclusion.) This effort aligns with trends in higher education toward more active and project-based pedagogies and suggests there may be valuable lessons to be learned from a course that embodies a cohesive mission in terms of outcomes, while retaining the flexibility to be offered in many different ways all across the country.

The ENACT model is *modular*. In fact, it *has* to be, in order for the diverse group of educators operating across different states to "plug in" to the network in ways that suit their localized contexts and institutional circumstances. This means that educators can choose which components make sense for them and their students. Perhaps specific assignments and elements of ENACT become a component of a larger course (or even an experience, such as an internship with a civic organization). Or perhaps the instructor chooses, as many of the authors of this volume have done, to organize an entire course around a suite of assignments and skill-building exercises that have emerged from dozens of scholars, over several years, experimenting with this approach. This modularity enables instructors to maintain flexibility and autonomy as they make these important decisions.

The ENACT program and model is highly *interdisciplinary*. While the model is an obvious fit for political science and public policy programs, Brandeis's ENACT network supports faculty from a wide range of departments and disciplinary specialties, including sociology and public policy, journalism and communication studies, and nursing and public health. In many of our courses, the students' interests in key issues facing their communities and states drive the legislation with which they will research and engage. State policymaking capacity continues to expand, offering numerous opportunities for student advocacy efforts on a range of policy issues. Any given legislative session is going to present a slew of policy questions that stretch across nearly every imaginable discipline and academic program. Thus, the ENACT framework can be adapted to align with nearly any major or course where the emphasis is on the development of practical, strategic communication skills and where the goal is to empower students to be more effective, thoughtful citizens.

Finally, beyond all of these instrumental reasons to take on the ENACT framework, ENACT is *fun*! The active approach of this course makes the material come alive in ways that even experiential methods such as a "simulation" simply would not be able to accomplish. Students may initially be intimidated by the prospect of engaging directly with policymakers and a bit mystified by policymaking processes that can be quite complex. However, they quickly become energized by the overlap between their roles as students and their emerging capacities as empowered citizens.

As an instructor in an ENACT course, you should not need to stridently make the case that the material matters; that regularly becomes self-evident to students. As a result, instructors who have adopted this model often return to it and become advocates for others to consider it (as evidenced by the authors of this text!). Students partaking in such a class gain valuable skills that set them on the path to professional success and give them the capacity to engage with the policymaking process as citizens, regardless of their eventual career path.

Who Should Read This Book?

This book is written with undergraduate instructors in mind, although from any discipline or any type of higher education institution. The ENACT network was built to work within this context, recruiting faculty fellows based at various colleges and universities across the country. All of this volume's authors are faculty fellows from that network, and so we focus here on faculty resources, needs, and considerations, while pointing to data that explores outcomes from the deployment of this course on a variety of campuses.

Still, there is reason to suspect that our overall argument here—that ENACT is adaptable to multiple circumstances in higher education—should extend to other contexts beyond higher ed. For example, ambitious K–12 teachers might consider incorporating an ENACT experience into a high school classroom. While there is little room in typical social studies curricula for such experiences, many secondary schools develop electives for social studies credit; ENACT could become a model for one such offering, or be incorporated into a broader civic engagement class. ENACT might also make a good plug-in project for other disciplines; perhaps a theater class might ask their state legislature for more arts funding, or aspiring engineers in a physics program might try to change a state's building code.

Similarly, ENACT might offer a model for advocacy training in the community, or at least some collaborative effort with educational institutions. A nonprofit leader or neighborhood activist looking to engage community members in advocacy might find useful ideas and information in these pages. While the formality of many assignments and rubrics might not be a good fit for such community contexts, the underlying principles and curricular approach can still apply to adult participants. Indeed, despite the focus on undergraduate education, a wide audience interested in advocacy will likely find something useful in this volume.

The Rest of the Book

The rest of this book offers a "how-to" guide on the components of ENACT. We will explain the major elements of an ENACT course, providing examples and sample assignments, and cover the risks and rewards that come along with implementation. We'll show how it all fits together, while providing readers with the flexibility they need to develop and implement the ENACT model in the way that best fits their institutional context and constraints.

Here is what you will find in the following pages:

- *Teaching an ENACT Course.* In this chapter, we offer some general guidance on the practical considerations related to teaching ENACT in different locations. States have varying rules and practices related to lawmaking as well as different legislative schedules, all of which impact course design. We offer questions to consider when designing ENACT courses to meet local conditions, as well as some initial resources to help with course planning.
- *Building Relationships at Your State Legislature.* Implementing the ENACT model requires more than just content expertise; success also depends on faculty's relationships, both at the state capitol and in their institution. In this chapter, we offer an overview for how to prepare for the course by making connections with people and resources at the state capitol. This often means building relationships with individual legislators, but also includes connecting with legislative librarians, nonpartisan research staff, revisor and legislation drafting offices, and legislative assistants and receptionists. Finally, we discuss how to minimize the political risks associated with teaching ENACT courses and build internal institutional support for the course. We share best practices that have emerged in the ENACT network for building buy-in, both within the legislature and at our colleges and universities.
- *Legislative Research.* ENACT courses require students to develop and practice research skills that are key elements of the higher education experience. In this chapter, we discuss considerations related to helping students choose bills based on student interest, cultural and legislative context, and the governing party's legislative agenda. We also suggest ways to prepare students to use the resources available at their institution and state capitol to contribute to their knowledge about their chosen bill. Depending on the state context, this can include accessing the legislature's website to track active legislation, accessing the legislative library and working with legislative librarians to learn about the history of their bill (or related bills), meeting with nonpartisan research staff in the House and/or the Senate, attending committee hearings, and meeting

with advocacy organizations to learn about lobbyists' and grassroots organizations' history of advocacy and messaging related to their bill. We also include an overview of a legislative research report assignment as well as an important artifact of advocacy work, the "one-pager." Finally, we address some of the key logistical questions instructors often have about guiding student bill selection.

- *Meeting with Legislators.* In ENACT courses, students meet with legislators to advocate on behalf of a particular bill; doing so effectively requires students to understand the cultural codes of the capitol and the norms of interaction. For many students, interacting with people in positions of power can promote feelings of anxiety and risk. In this chapter, we discuss strategies to build student confidence and demystify the legislature (and legislators), so students feel empowered to advocate for their bills. We discuss the importance of explicit instruction on both institutional norms and historical context and provide guidance related to helping students make strategic decisions about self-presentation and communication at the capitol. This chapter also includes an overview of key assignments to prepare for meetings, including the elevator speech and meeting script, and more contextual activities that range from a panel discussion with legislators to an alternative capitol tour.
- *Engaging with the Public.* Advocacy sometimes requires more than just persuasive meetings with legislators and can depend on the ability to win support from the broader community. In this chapter, we discuss communication strategies for effectively engaging the public. We suggest to students how they can use letters to the editor, opinion pieces, and social media to build public support for their bills. We provide guidance for involving local policy experts in the course as guest speakers to prepare students to develop impactful public arguments. We also share ideas for creative social media assignments, which allow students to connect with their peers and community members to invite them to support their advocacy work. This chapter also includes an overview of public-facing assignments like an op-ed, as well as suggestions for how to contact advocacy organizations.
- *Life after ENACT.* Completing the legislative advocacy project is a huge accomplishment for students. In this chapter, we discuss multiple options for celebrating those accomplishments. In some ENACT

courses, students test their advocacy against critique through a present and defend activity, while in others students discuss broader reflections on democracy as part of a community celebration. Concluding activities provide students with the opportunity to reflect on their work and solidify their learning. We suggest considerations that might lead an educator to choose one type of event over the other. We also offer guidance for how to extend students' participation in advocacy work after the course ends, through joining grassroots organizations, becoming members of advocacy organizations, and/or pursuing work in politics.

- *Conclusion.* In a brief concluding chapter, we discuss again why ENACT matters and provide evidence as to how it prepares students for active political participation throughout their lives. We discuss findings about the effectiveness of ENACT courses for encouraging civic-mindedness, increasing participation among students, and as a means for restoring student faith in democratic institutions. In addition, we share what ENACT has meant to us as educators and how it has positively impacted and influenced our teaching practices more generally. We end with an invitation to readers to try teaching the ENACT model and see how it impacts their students and themselves.

Each of the chapters that cover these major elements is organized into four sections, aimed at addressing the considerations an instructor might need to take into account when designing a new course or student experience:

- What are the *key questions* to consider when adapting the ENACT model to your individual instructional context?
- What are some of the *assignments and other course components* you might consider including? Here we reference sample assignment guidelines, worksheets, and (occasionally) rubrics that are included at the back of each chapter.
- What are some *additional resources*—campus offices, off-campus connections, networks, literature, or anything else—that might help you implement this ENACT component?
- What are some *examples of guidelines, assignments, and student submissions* that can serve as models for you as you develop and implement your own ENACT course?

· In order to help reinforce the student focus of the ENACT experience, each chapter includes quotes from students who have participated in ENACT courses to help illuminate their experiences.

We believe that all of these materials should be seen as a point of departure. Faculty decisions about what to emphasize on assignments and how to assess them will vary greatly. You should feel free to borrow the components that work best for you, remix them if necessary, and build a course in a way that supports your learning goals, institutional structure, legislature, and student population.

After reading this book, you should feel ready to make the ENACT model your own. You will be able to empower yourself, your institution, and—most importantly—your students to go forth and ENACT change.

> *Since taking Advocacy for Policy Change, I have a much better understanding of how my state legislature functions, who the representatives are, how to access information about legislation important to me, and how to effectively communicate my preferences to the appropriate political actors. I also learned how to find local advocacy groups working on the issues I am interested in, which enabled me to build meaningful relationships with like-minded people, furthered my education on how to be an involved citizen, and further amplified my political voice.*
>
> GAIL MILLER, Metropolitan State University, Minnesota

NOTES

1. APSA Task Force on Civic Education in the 21st Century, "Expanded Articulation Statement: A Call for Reactions and Contributions," *PS: Political Science & Politics* 31, no. 1 (March 1998): 636–38.

2. John R. Hibbing and Elizabeth Theiss-Morse, *Stealth Democracy: Americans' Beliefs About How Government Should Work* (Cambridge: Cambridge University Press, 2002); Colin Hay, *Why We Hate Politics* (Cambridge, UK: Polity Press, 2007).

3. Jennifer Jerit and Yangzi Zhao, "Political Misinformation," *Annual Review of Political Science* 23, no. 1 (May 2020): 77–94.

4. Amy Fried and Douglas B. Harris, *At War with Government: How Conservatives Weaponized Distrust from Goldwater to Trump* (New York: Columbia University Press, 2021).

5. Karen O'Brien, Elin Selboe, and Bronwyn M. Hayward, "Exploring Youth Activism on Climate Change: Dutiful, Disruptive, and Dangerous Dissent," *Ecology and Society* 23, no. 3 (October 2018), https://doi.org/10.5751/ES-10287-230342.

6. Christine Emeran, "The March for Our Lives Movement in the United States: Generational Change and the Personalization of Protest," in *When Students Protest: Secondary and High Schools*, ed. Judith Bessant, Analicia Mejia Mesinas, and Sarah Pickard (Lanham, MD: Rowman & Littlefield, 2021), 145–60.

7. Arielle Baskin-Sommers et al., "Adolescent Civic Engagement: Lessons from Black Lives Matter," *Proceedings of the National Academy of Sciences* 118, no. 41 (December 2021), www.pnas.org/content/118/41/e2109860118.

8. J. Cherie Strachan, "Student and Civic Engagement: Cultivating the Skills, Efficacy and Identities That Increase Student Involvement in Learning and in Public Life," in *Handbook on Teaching and Learning in Political Science and International Relations*, ed. John Ishiyama, William J. Miller, and Eszter Simon (Northampton, MA: Edward Elgar, 2015), 145–60.

9. Elizabeth A. Bennion and Xander E. Laughlin, "Best Practices in Civic Education: Lessons from the *Journal of Political Science Education*," *Journal of Political Science Education* 14, no. 3 (January 2018): 287–330; Lauren C. Bell, Allison Rank, and Carah Ong Whaley, ed., *Civic Pedagogies: Teaching Civic Engagement in an Era of Divisive Politics* (New York: Palgrave Macmillan, 2024).

10. "ENACT: The Educational Network for Active Civic Transformation," ENACT, accessed July 1, 2024, www.brandeis.edu/enact.

11. "Program Components," ENACT, accessed July 1, 2024, www.brandeis.edu/enact/program-components.html.

12. Robert W. Glover, Kathleen Cole, and Katharine Owens, "ENACT-ing Leadership at the State Level: A National Educational Network for Engaged Citizenship in State Legislatures," *Maine Policy Review* 27, No. 1 (2018): 22–26; Robert W. Glover et al., "Advocating for Engagement: Do Experiential Learning Courses Boost Civic Engagement?" *Journal of Political Science Education* 17, Supp. 1 (2021): 599–615.

1 Teaching an ENACT Course

TAKING ON ANY active learning experience can be a challenge for instructors. There may sometimes be little incentive to build additional learning models into your classes. Leaving aside faculty workloads, the "Sage on the Stage" model of lectures, homework, and exams has a long history in higher education. Moreover, this traditional model is so institutionalized in our educational system that it is often rewarded; student evaluations reflect their comfort level with a talented and entertaining lecturer, and administrators are often placated with a smoothly run semester with no hiccups. Why upset the applecart by trying to vary student experiences or, worse, taking students outside of the classroom?

Still, the experience of many instructors—and a growing body of literature, supported by extensive data[1]—shows how valuable active learning encounters are for students. Faculty may recognize this, however, and still have well-justified concerns about the risks involved: Do you have the resources to support this effort? Do you have the time in your class? Is such an effort even feasible under current institutional and environmental circumstances?

The good news is that the ENACT course offers an exceedingly flexible model. ENACT allows for—and even encourages—adaptation to local circumstances, both the institution and the instructor's resources and inclinations. ENACT has been successfully taught in a variety of contexts under various constraints. We argue that in almost all circumstances you should see an ENACT course as not only feasible but also rewarding for both student and teacher.

Below we address some of the major considerations you should review while considering how to implement an ENACT course.

Key Questions

What are the institutional features of your campus and class setting that may affect how you implement the ENACT model?

ENACT is, as noted throughout this book, exceedingly adaptable. Such flexibility is important due to the sheer variety of institutional contexts. While all college educators could be considered to be engaged in largely the same project, institutional variety makes that project look very different in your home institution as compared to ours. You should consider some of the following features of your institutional setting when developing an ENACT course experience.

- *Student makeup.* An important question for the instructor in any class is: Who are your students? You are hopefully familiar with demographic features of your student body as a whole and have considered how the features and identities of students factor into the classroom. Still, questions of race, class, gender, sexuality, citizenship status, and other factors of identity and community background might be even more salient as you enter into active engagement with your state's outside political environment. We especially encourage you to think about how to account for such factors while still keeping the ENACT experience open to as many interested students as possible. (See chapter 4 for a discussion of how such factors might impact ENACT course planning.)

  Another important consideration is the knowledge base of your particular students. Some ENACT classes are designed with advanced political science majors in mind, while others are more wide-ranging experiences open to students of different skill levels and disciplinary backgrounds. Even some of those students majoring in politics may be unfamiliar with state government institutions. To help ensure a shared knowledge base, you could require prerequisites, although this can of course prevent some interested students from participating.
- *Class logistics.* You should consider some basic features of course design for this specific class. How many students are you expecting/are enrolled? Instructors who regularly implement active learning exercises will note that running such complicated experiences in large university classes with dozens of participants can be hard, although not impossible, to

manage. Similarly, what is the timing of the class: a full semester, or just a monthlong summer or break-based experience? Or, if the course unfolds over a full semester, can you devote the entire class to ENACT or not? Finally, what is the modality of course delivery? Online courses can incorporate various ENACT elements, although in-person courses still present the best opportunity for full engagement.

- *Resources.* Since this course encourages visits to the state capitol, what resources are available for transportation? If students are expected to travel on their own, what kinds of policies are in place to govern required student travel? Some of the activities and exercises described within might require additional supplies and services, particularly food and beverages. Do you have a departmental or institutional budget to support even small print jobs, snacks, or meals?

  More broadly, does your institution offer supportive training and professional development resources that can help scaffold active learning experiences like ENACT? While ENACT is a unique model, it can incorporate many active learning pedagogies, including project-based learning and basic group exercise techniques. Institutions that have a center for teaching and learning can be helpful resources to guide instructors.

What are the institutional features of your political environment that may affect how you implement the ENACT model?

Looking outward beyond the campus walls, you should consider the key features of the political environment, particularly the target institution for the ENACT experience: the state legislature. Lawmaking bodies vary as much as states themselves do, ranging from full-time, "professionalized" legislatures working year-round in states like California and Massachusetts to part-time assemblies that may only meet every other year, as in North Dakota and Montana. Some of the institutional features you might consider include the following:

- *Accessibility.* Some legislatures have become more professionalized, with full-time salaries and staff resources modeled on Congress. Others follow the "citizen-legislator" model, where part-time lawmakers are expected to maintain a foothold in the "real world" in order to better represent their constituents. Whatever the merits of the latter model, it does present some challenges to instructors in terms of scheduling. Will legislators be in session during your class?

In the following chapters, we will recommend that you get students into the legislative space as much as possible. Still, geographic distance is a key factor; not all state capitals are conveniently located next to your campus, and vice versa. For example, there are over two dozen colleges located in San Diego, California, but students there would need to complete an *eight-hour* drive up the coast to visit the state capitol in Sacramento. Multiple visits, or even a single visit, may prove daunting depending on how far away your classroom is from the seat of government.

Still, you should note that while legislative advocacy visits are a key part of ENACT, even these can be modified or adapted to your local circumstances. Legislators often make decisions about which bills to support and carry before the legislature is in session, and so advocacy visits with local legislators can take place in their districts at any time throughout the year. (In fact, some representatives recommend such visits, as they have more time to speak with students outside of a hectic session.) Virtual visits can make connecting with other legislators across the state a possibility. Don't let a poorly aligned calendar or an inconvenient map prevent you from considering or implementing this model!

· *Politics and demographics.* Navigating legislative politics in many states has become more challenging in recent years. Legislatures have always reflected entrenched networks, but now ideological conflicts are exacerbated and fed by the nationalization of state politics. We discuss the importance of navigating the specific cultural and political context of your state legislature in chapter 3, but you may want to be aware of any obstacles or challenge points in the political environment as you consider course design as well.

Similarly, the demographics of the legislature may impact your design. The makeup of the legislature may not be representative on a variety of dimensions—of the state population, the population in your local community, or your specific student body. Such dynamics of representation offer additional challenges for course design, particularly for students who may encounter difficulty with feeling a sense of belonging in possibly alienating spaces. (See chapter 4.)

> *Without the ENACT program at Brandeis University, I would have never had the political and advocacy experience I now have.... ENACT has helped inspire me to learn more about what I am passionate about, and has taught me that anyone can raise their voice and make a difference!*
>
> Sage Rosenthal, Brandeis University

How will you structure the course calendar?

How much ENACT do you want or need? Is this a full ENACT class, focused entirely on the legislative advocacy process? Or is this a specific class with a disciplinary role or purpose that will have an ENACT experience built into it? While it is certainly possible to support a full ENACT class, many ENACT instructors have instead "imported" ENACT into other contexts, ranging from a classic state government political science class to more specialized policy and politics classes in fields like nursing or environmental studies.

Decisions about how to structure an ENACT course may depend on some of the logistical constraints noted above. Is the state legislature nearby and in session, enabling sustained engagement at the capitol? Other constraints will be related to your specific disciplinary needs. If you are incorporating the ENACT experience within an existing or otherwise "regular" course, that course's learning objectives may constrain the amount of time you can spend on an ENACT project. If students need to study state institutions or healthcare policy and practice, they may only have a few selected classes to devote to the ENACT components described throughout this volume.

Finally, one additional kind of academic experience often connects to, and even overlaps with, the ENACT experience: that of an academic internship. University internship programs may include experiences in and around the state legislature. ENACT instructors have often found the ENACT experience to be helpful in preparing for such internships, and have even combined or connected these experiences. For example, a student could participate in an internship while enrolled in an ENACT course or complete an internship before or after ENACT. While certainly not required, these combinations suggest additional creative possibilities through which ENACT can be deployed in your curriculum.

For example, at the University of Hartford, many students who have taken ENACT-focused classes serve as interns for the Connecticut General Assembly, and students who have already interned in the General Assembly take ENACT classes. When students in ENACT classes have already served as interns, this cross-pollination improves classroom discussions about policy issues and the general workings of the legislature. These students have firsthand experience working in the legislature that they share with their classmates. At other times, students in ENACT classes then apply for the legislative internship; this allows students with previous experience in writing policy briefs, op-eds, and storycards to share these skills as interns for legislators. In other cases, students who have taken ENACT classes have been selected for internships with public relations and lobbying firms that specialize in the legislature or with advocacy organizations in labor rights, environment, and other policy issues.

> *I am much more confident and assertive when speaking with authority figures. I gained a better understanding of how to advocate for things I care about.*
>
> —from a survey of Brandeis alumni who participated in ENACT course

How will your students work together?

ENACT courses almost always encourage students to collaborate in groups, for at least two reasons. First, the advocacy experience is rarely a solo enterprise, as advocacy coalitions, lobbyists, and other interested parties often find themselves on the same side of a bill. Second, as with many active learning experiences, the ENACT advocacy project is an excellent opportunity to help students develop general collaboration skills. The original Brandeis model favors pairing up students, but other instructors work with larger groups. Your comfort level and familiarity with group work can govern the ENACT experience. Still, you might consider a few basic questions:

- How do you wish to structure groups? Pairs or larger groups? Varied or uniform group sizes?
- Do you wish to allow students to choose their own partners, or assign

them? Students can build collaboration skills by working with unfamiliar faces but may be more comfortable working with those they know. You can sort students by their choice of bill or policy area as well.

- Will you assess collaboration skills as part of assignments? There are widely available rubrics for group work that can be incorporated into assessments or used separately.[2]
- How will you settle conflict? Some instructors may offer rules and guidelines for group work, while others may ask students to develop their own.

None of these kinds of questions is particularly specific to ENACT, and so you may already have the infrastructure developed for group work that can just be incorporated into your ENACT class. Still, you might consider different ways of getting groups to think about working together in the advocacy context. Later in this chapter, we offer guidelines for one approach to organizing students into groups, focused on an initial proposal that outlines group rules and logistics. And in chapter 4, we describe an ongoing "check-in" assignment for you to help manage and support your students' group activities and communication.

What are some strategies to address institutional hesitancy or discomfort about your students' direct engagement with lawmakers?

ENACT classes are unique and will typically involve students engaging in evidence-based advocacy for or against a piece of public policy. Many of your students will choose issues that impact them directly. This makes them ideal policy messengers with "lived experience" that can enrich the policymaking process—exactly the types of voices that the legislature ought to seek out.

With that said, universities jealously protect their institutional reputations and are intentional in the relationships they cultivate with lawmakers and the institutional positions they adopt on matters of public policy. Most universities, therefore, will have a policy that stipulates that speaking as a student or a faculty member should not be construed as a formal policy statement from the university. You should certainly remind students of such policies as they participate in advocacy, because it protects their work—and yours—from the need for any interference from university authorities. Nevertheless, as you develop and plan your course, university administrators (department chairs, deans, provosts, governmental relations staff, etc.) may still be concerned about interactions with the state legislature over which they do not have direct control.

Typically, such fears stem from imagining the course as a more confrontational form of activism, where a hostile encounter between students and lawmakers will require the university's external relations staff to engage in some form of "damage control." As you will see throughout this text, the course empowers students to engage in nonpartisan, evidence-based, civil, and respectful policy advocacy. Though legislative advocacy is an important component of political activism, the course encourages students to engage within existing political institutions, rather than disrupting or obstructing them. Frequently, once administrators see the way that the course actually operates, they recognize the positive ways that it outwardly represents their students as thoughtful, engaged, serious participants in our democracy. In most cases of our existing ENACT courses, departments and institutions become enthusiastic promoters and advocates for the course, often seeking to publicize it in their external communications and marketing materials.

To facilitate this process, it may be advisable to proactively invite such individuals into the course. If the university has a governmental relations staff person or a communications team, schedule a class session in which they join your class and share insights from their own work building relationships. If the university president or provost goes before lawmakers to testify about the importance of research funding or investment in higher education, reach out to ask them to share their expertise and insights with your students. On the other hand, attempting to "fly under the radar" can leave administrators or public relations staff feeling blindsided or misled when they learn that university students and faculty are engaging directly with lawmakers. Those who regularly teach these courses have found that being transparent and keeping university administrators fully aware of the type of innovative and exciting pedagogical work you are doing is the best strategy to generate institutional buy-in.

Assignments and Other Key Course Components

Syllabus

Instructors know well the frustrations of students asking basic questions or lacking knowledge about course structure and assignments only to tell them, often with frustration, "It's in the syllabus!" Still, as much as some students resist it, the syllabus is a crucial document for a course, as it essentially tells the story of the term. It can be as important for the instructor as the students; even if the class community tends to overlook the document after the first day of class, just the act of creation can help you plan how the semester will run—or at least how you *hope* it will run.

The syllabus serves the same purpose for an ENACT course. Still, you might incorporate some of the following considerations as you write the syllabus and, concurrently, plan the course:

- *Course structure.* Many of the key structural concerns noted above—logistics, travel, accessibility, etc.—will be reflected in the syllabus, and especially the course schedule. How will your particular course specifically navigate all of these factors?
- *Readings/assignments.* As also noted above, your students may vary in their knowledge about state government and politics more generally. How much attention do you need or wish to pay to building up students' vocabulary and knowledge base? You could read parts of a standard textbook designed for state government courses. There are accessible narrative books about legislative policymaking as well.[3]
- *Risks.* As with any course that asks students to step outside the classroom, there are risks involved in the activities described here. Your institution may have required language for field trips and off-campus assignments. You may also consider including your own language in the syllabus that might be designed to assuage students' concerns and questions. Certainly, you don't need to overstate or overemphasize risks to the point of scaring students away from the course! Still, the syllabus should indicate just what students are getting themselves into and at least point to any accompanying downsides.
- *Learning objectives.* As noted above, how much ENACT is there in your course? How much do these ENACT objectives have to coexist with other needs of the course, including disciplinary requirements?

You will find sample course schedules with varied options along with course descriptions, as well as sample learning objectives, at the end of this chapter.

Current Events/Issues Review

In order to build knowledge of your particular state government's policies and politics, you might consider including some basic participation assignments for the term. One option is to assign a "current events" or "current issues" review or brief, where students review news sources about state government and submit or post a discussion of a current bill or other aspect of state politics. Weekly or daily reviews of such discussion briefs can help quickly bring the class up to speed on the key issues being discussed in your state legislature. Sample assignment guidelines are included at the end of this chapter, and some resources that may be helpful for such an assignment are also included later in this chapter.

Additional Resources

There are a number of resources that can scaffold your ENACT experience, located both on campus and off.

Literature and Research

As noted above, there is a growing interdisciplinary literature on active learning, covering a host of interventions and techniques from a variety of pedagogical approaches, ranging from experiential learning to project- or problem-based learning to design thinking or design-based learning. For example, PBLWorks (formerly the Buck Institute for Education) offers a number of free resources for project-based learning approaches, including strategies, exercises, and rubrics.[4]

Some universities also offer active learning resources to the public; for instance, Harvard's Derek Bok Center for Teaching and Learning publishes ABLConnect,[5] an "activity-based learning" hub with exercises and guides to the literature on a number of different modalities.

Local/State News Sources

Local news sources and journalists are essential resources for you and your students in following the latest issues being discussed in your state legislature. Newspapers, television and radio stations, and news websites can provide varying levels of coverage.

Seeking out such sources becomes more challenging in today's media environment, where structural changes such as corporate consolidation and the collapse of classified ads have accelerated the collapse of local media outlets, particularly newspapers. If you live in a "news desert"[6] without much coverage of state legislation, you may have difficulty immersing students in state politics. Still, there may be alternative news sources, such as local bloggers or "citizen journalists" who report on government meetings and issues. Some states even have nonprofit newsletters and aggregators[7] that share the day's or week's big stories; you can subscribe and/or ask your students to subscribe while they are enrolled in your class.

State Legislature Websites

The official website of your state legislature can be an invaluable resource for you and your students—not just for providing a legislative database to track bills (see chapter 3), but also just to help you all learn more about your state legislature and how it operates. Some states, like Virginia[8] and Nevada,[9] publish printed guides to the legislature. (Nevada updates theirs every other year!) Other states offer more dynamic and interactive guides on their websites.[10]

ENACT Platform

The ENACT program at Brandeis University offers a digital platform[11] that organizes resources from ENACT faculty fellows, including syllabi, assignments, and sample student products. The platform has been used by network organizers to support faculty fellows, but Brandeis has made most of the materials available to the public. While we have provided samples and "ideal types" for assignment guidelines in this book, you can seek out additional models and varieties here as well.

Faculty and Staff Colleagues

Finally, you should consider what resources you may find among your colleagues on campus. If you are coming to ENACT from a discipline or research perspective that is not regularly engaged with the state legislature, you might have a colleague who is much more connected. Reach out to faculty who teach in political science and/or state government or who might be quoted in local news stories about state legislation. Seek out on-campus staff with a role that might bring them into contact with state legislators and their support staff, such as your university's government relations office. As suggested above, you might consider even bringing these colleagues into your class as a guest speaker, if appropriate.

Conclusion

Any active learning technique requires careful planning and consideration. The following chapters will fill out the details of the overview and schedule offered in this chapter. Still, while this chapter offered a lot of these considerations, we encourage you to avoid getting caught up in details in a way that prevents you from adopting this course model. Remember, you can feel free to pilot aspects of the model in your classes. We offer a complete model in these pages, but you should feel free to start small and move further into the model as you go along.

Sample Course Descriptions

Course Description 1: ENACT Course

This course is an experiential exploration of state politics and policymaking.

A society's laws will generally reflect widely accepted notions of what is ethical behavior and what will best protect the public good. Sometimes, there is wide disagreement about the ethical or moral value of a particular law. Recent examples include the heated debates surrounding the legalization of gay marriage, the abolition of the juvenile death penalty, the right to die, abortion, the ban of assault weapons, and the path to citizenship. More historic examples include challenges to women's suffrage and the legality of racial segregation laws, the overturning of which now seem to our society as unquestionably right.

This course combines an investigation of the ethical dilemmas that arise in the process of lawmaking with hands-on advocacy work. Students will be encouraged to think deeply about the complexities of shaping laws for constituents who hold diverse viewpoints and how best to progress through the legislative process.

The course will begin by exploring a number of situations where lawmaking and ethical beliefs of some sector of the US public have been in conflict. What has been the role of lawmakers as well as the greater public in the promotion of new laws that redress perceived wrongs or shortcomings? Should democracy always rule or is there a role for enlightened leaders to take charge of social progress in the face of broad public disapproval? Most importantly, what role does advocacy play in enacting social change through legislation?

Therefore, this will be a "hands-on" course: students will carry out, in real time, an applied advocacy project that takes the things we read and talk about in political science classes and puts them into practice. More specifically, students will work in teams to identify a bill currently before the state legislature and develop and execute a step-by-step plan for helping to get that bill enacted or defeated.

Course Description 2: ENACT Experience within State Government Course

When we talk about government, we often focus on the national level, thinking of the president's latest tweet, a congressional vote, or a supreme court case. Yet *subnational governments*—the fifty US states, and the thousands of city, county, and municipal governments that operate within their borders—affect our lives just as much, if not more. Citizens engage with state and/or local governments whenever they take a driver's test, try to get a pothole fixed on their street, or send their kids to public schools. It is in our daily lives and day-to-day interactions with these governments and their representatives (police officers, case workers, bureaucrats, etc.) that we truly experience the results of policies and politics. And yet these governments are overlooked, understudied, and quite possibly undervalued by the majority of Americans.

In the context of our particular state, we will explore *the nature of American government and politics at the subnational level.* This exploration includes lectures, activities, exams, and a *hands-on advocacy project* where students will engage directly in advocating for laws in the state legislature. By the end of the course, students should have a better understanding of what these subnational governments do and how important they are.

Course Description 3: ENACT Experience within Interdisciplinary Course (Healthcare Policy)

The American Medical Association defines healthcare as a "fundamental human good." Healthcare is also a pressing political, ethical, and legal issue that requires a number of government laws, rules, and regulations in order to ensure adequate, efficient, and equitable delivery of healthcare services to the public. "Healthcare policy" is the umbrella term for all of these governmental interventions in healthcare, and it can cover anything from federal rules for Medicare payments to a local school district's immunization requirements.

This course will provide an overview of American healthcare policy. We will discuss some major aspects of national healthcare policy, including public health and nutrition, mental health policy, and funding issues. For the final project in the course, we will focus on the state level, engaging in a real-time advocacy project that will identify current healthcare bills in the state legislature and advocate for their passage.

Students should leave this course with a better understanding of the way that the healthcare system works—and, hopefully, a sense of how they might work to reform it for the better.

Sample Learning Objectives

Some suggested learning objectives relating specifically to ENACT courses and/or ENACT course components:

Knowledge-Based Learning Objectives

- Acquire an understanding of the significant role state and local governments play in the US federalist system
- Understand the institutions, politics, processes, and services of state and local governments

- Recognize the many actors and stakeholders who take part in the state policy process
- Articulate the process by which laws do (or do not) become enacted in your state

Skills-Based Learning Objectives

- Communicate your policy expertise in a variety of oral, written, and visual forms, across multiple settings, for diverse audiences
- Develop and demonstrate expertise in a specific policy area in state politics
- Identify, develop, and demonstrate strategies used to advocate for policy change

Big-Picture/Reflective Learning Objectives

- Explain some of the circumstances under which citizens and advocacy organizations might affect the state policymaking process
- Grasp and articulate the challenges of achieving justice through legislation
- Acknowledge and reflect upon your role as a citizen in a representative democracy

Sample Course Schedules

Course Schedule 1: Full Semester Outline

Tuesday, January 16

- The role of the citizen advocate and the advocacy power prism
- The legislative process

Tuesday, January 23

- Introduction to the Marriage Equality Campaign with Maxine Isaacs, co-chair of the State LGTBQ+ Caucus for Change
- Complete advocacy for policy change interest form

Tuesday, January 30

- Meet the advocacy organizations (guest speakers)
- Introduction to legislative advocacy projects and ENACT
- Obtain the bill, the factsheet, and section-by-section summary of your bill; identify contact information and background of two legislative sponsors of your bill
- Collect the contact information and description of two coalition organizations
- Present interview plan for preparation storybook assignment

Tuesday, February 6

- Discuss lessons learned from advocacy readings
- Rules for influencing policymakers
- Schedule interviews and begin interviewing in preparation for storybook draft

Tuesday, February 13

- Meet with bill sponsors at statehouse
- Legislative research report due Friday, February 16

Tuesday, February 27

- Develop a compelling message
- ENACT student panel on tips for success
- Storybook draft due; present in class
- Legislative meeting plan for March 12 statehouse visit

Tuesday, March 5

- Storybook final due
- Present elevator speech in class

Tuesday, March 12

- Statehouse lobbying session 1 (meet at main entrance by 9:30 a.m.)
- Elevator speech, letter to legislator, and monologue to House Ways and Means due
- Due after class: write thank you notes/follow-up emails to legislators/staffers

Tuesday, March 19
- Media advocacy: the op-ed
- Video activism
- Legislative meeting plan for April 2 statehouse visit due

Tuesday, March 26
- Policymaking through the budget process with State Representative Subramanyam
- Media advocacy op-ed due

Tuesday, April 2
- Statehouse lobbying session 2 (meet at main entrance by 9:30 a.m.)
- Campaign journal due Friday, April 5, at 5:00 p.m.
- Due after class: write thank you notes/follow-up emails to legislators/staffers

Tuesday, April 9
- Prepare for present and defend legislative advocacy project (present "draft" in class)
- Media advocacy video due

Tuesday, April 16
- Present and defend
- Reflection and conclusion
- Final written advocacy portfolio due

Course Schedule 2: One-Month Term

Week 1 (January 5–9): LEARN
- Monday: In-class introduction
- Tuesday: Orientation at the capitol (optional)
- Wednesday: Crash course in state government
- Thursday: Shadow advocacy day at capitol (optional)
- Friday: Getting organized

Week 2 (January 12–16): RESEARCH
· Monday: Bills workshop
· Tuesday: Research workshop
· Wednesday: Advocacy skills
· Thursday: Legislative research reports (in-class group presentations)
· Friday: NO CLASS (use time to schedule advocacy visits)

Week 3 (January 19–23): ADVOCATE
· Monday: Advocacy meeting simulations/practice
· Tuesday–Friday: Advocacy visits at capitol

Week 4 (January 26–30): REFLECT
· Monday: Final advocacy visits
· Tuesday: Debrief/check-ins
· Wednesday: Presentation walk-throughs
· Thursday: Lessons learned presentations and wrap-up
· Friday: NO CLASS (final papers/reports due)

Course Schedule 3: ENACT Experience within State Government Course

Week 1 (February 14–16): Introduction
· Course overview
· Importance of state and local politics

Weeks 2–3 (February 21–March 2): State Government
· Federalism
· Constitutions
· State policy workshop

Weeks 4–7 (March 7–30): State Institutions
· Legislatures
· Governors
· Courts
· Bureaucracy
· Parties and interest groups
· Introduction to advocacy project

SPRING BREAK: April 4–8

Weeks 8–11 (April 11–May 4): Local Politics

- Types of local government
- State-local relations
- Regionalism
- Advocacy project workshops

Week 12 (May 9–11): Policy Change

- Advocacy visits

Week 13 (May 16–18): Next Steps

- Reflection presentations
- Wrap-up and next steps

Monday, May 22, 5 p.m.: Final legislative research reports due

Week	Date	Topic	Assigned Course Materials	Assignments Due
1	1/11	Introduction to the course: Overview of the course; students join legislative advocacy teams; overview of legislators, bills, and committees. Attendance mandatory for first day of class because we will be choosing teams that day!	None.	None.
2	1/18	Politics Is about Power: Discussion of the difference between politics for power and politics for personal expression; discussion of the conditions shaping this legislative session; overview of the legislative process. Class visit from the revisor's office.	Hirsch, selections from *Politics Is for Power*; selected local news articles.	Reading response paper 1 due; issue selection assignment due.
3	1/25	Legislatures as Public Problem Solving Spaces: Capitol tour; meeting with legislators to discuss their connections to their communities and theories of representation; legislative library tour. Class visit to the state capitol.	Rosenthal, chapters 1 and 2.	Reading response paper 2 due.

Table 1. Course Schedule 4: Full-Semester Grid.

Continued⟶

Week	Date	Topic	Assigned Course Materials	Assignments Due
4	2/1	Who Has Power, Who Gets Represented?: Discussions of politics as conflict resolution and community creation; why people in the US dislike democracy; why people run for office; descriptive representation and state legislatures; barriers to candidacy for various demographic groups and impact on policy outcomes.	Reingold, "Gender, Race/ Ethnicity, and Representation in State Legislatures"; Bhojwani, selections from *People Like Us*.	Reading response paper 3 due.
5	2/8	Legislators as Representatives of Districts and Parties: Discussions of various ways that legislators act on behalf of their constituents; the relationship between legislators and their party; the importance of majority control.	Rosenthal, chapters 3 and 4.	Reading response paper 4 due.
6	2/15	Lobbying the Legislature: Discussion of interest groups and lobbyists' roles in the legislative process; class visit from lobbyist Anthony Kahn and organizer Marilyn Cohen; overview of scheduling your meetings with legislators.	Rosenthal chapter 5; Manos, "9 Ways to Approach Congressional Staffers to Get Your Issue Heard."	Reading response paper 5 due.
7	2/22	Making Your Case in the Media: Discussion of op-eds and their impact on the policymaking process; class visit from Fatima Al-Bahar, editorial board of the *Star Dispatch* newspaper.	Indivisible and the Op-Ed Project, "Writing Op-Eds That Make a Difference."	Legislative research report first draft due.
8	3/1	Workshopping Letters to the Editor: Students will bring their draft letters to class for peer review.	None.	Letter to the editor first draft due.
Spring Break	3/8		Enjoy your break!	
9	3/15	The Governor in the Legislative Process: Discussion of the role of the governor's office in the legislative process; class visit from Anthony Santinez, deputy policy director for the governor; overview of preparing for a successful meeting with a legislator.	Rosenthal, chapter 8; Boniface, "10 Strategies to Successfully Brief a Hill Staffer or Lawmaker."	Reading response paper 6 due;letter to the editor final draft due.

Table 1. Course Schedule 4: Full-Semester Grid.

Continued→

Week	Date	Topic	Assigned Course Materials	Assignments Due
10	3/22	Workshopping Elevator Speeches and Meeting Scripts: Students will bring their draft elevator speeches and meeting scripts to class for peer review.	None.	Elevator speech first draft due; meeting script first draft due; one-pager first draft due.
11	3/29	Law and Lawmaking: Discussion of the enabling and constraining conditions that impact the policymaking process.	Rosenthal, chapters 9 and 10.	Reading response paper 7 due;one-pager final draft due.
12	4/5	Lobbying Legislators: Students visit the capitol for meetings with legislators. Students without meetings scheduled will work in the legislative library or attend committee hearings with instructor.	None.	Elevator speech and meeting script final draft due.
13	4/12	Lobbying Legislators: Students visit the capitol for meetings with legislators. Students without meetings scheduled will work in the legislative library or attend committee hearings with instructor.	None.	None.
14	4/19	Using Your Power: Reflection on what it means to use power and advocate on behalf of our communities; consideration of other democratic skills necessary for representing the interests of ordinary people in state government; how to give public presentations on policy.	Mitchell, "Building Resilient Organizations."	Reading response paper 8 due; draft Final Presentation due.
15	4/26	Final Presentations: Students present their legislative advocacy projects to the class and guests.	None.	Legislative Research Report final draft due; Final Presentation due.

Sample Assignment Guidelines for Group Proposal

Two tips students should know about completing project work:

- Research projects often require a *proposal* (for funding, for acceptance at a conference or as part of a book, etc.).
- Larger projects in general require *planning*.

To encourage you to engage in planning, I ask you to submit the following elements as part of a research proposal:

1. Logistics

Write up a brief "prenup" agreement. (Just as some marriage participants ask their partners to sign a prenuptial contract before the "nuptials" or mar-

Week	Date	Readings	In Class Work and Assignment Schedule
1	8/29	Introduction to the course.	Learn about state legislature; discuss policy areas and interests.
2	9/5	Stone, chapter 1, "The Market and the Polis." Stone, chapter 2, "Goals: Equity." Topic reading: Climate change.	Form groups; legislative bill search; select bill for semester.
3	9/12	Stone, chapter 3, "Goals: Efficiency." Topic readings: Federal land use policy, fracking.	Discuss policy brief assignment; share sample policy briefs.
4	9/19	Stone, chapter 4, "Goals: Security." Stone, chapter 5, "Goals: Liberty." Topic readings: Education: Mississippi, death penalty.	
5	9/26	Stone, chapter 6, "Problems: Symbols." Stone, chapter 7, "Problems: Numbers." Topic readings: Gun control, gender pay gap.	Policy brief due; share sample storycards.
6	10/3	Guest speaker: State representative.	
7	10/10	Stone, chapter 8, "Problems: Causes." Stone, chapter 9, "Problems: Interests." Topic readings: American elections, gerrymandering, child labor.	Storycard assignment due; discuss legislative research report assignment; share sample legislative research reports.

Table 2. Course Schedule 5: ENACT Course When Legislature Is Not in Session. *Continued→*

riage, I ask you to draw up and sign an agreement before moving forward on your work together.) Prenups should include the following:

- Identify team roles as appropriate
  - Will you have a team leader? Will you have specific areas of responsibility?
  - Lay out some logistics about how team members will work together (communication, meeting times, etc.)
- Explain how teams will resolve any differences that may arise
  - What happens if someone doesn't meet deadlines and/or shirks responsibility?
- Agreement (indicate in some way that everyone in the group has "signed on" and agreed to these terms)

Week	Date	Readings	In Class Work and Assignment Schedule
8	10/17	Stone, chapter 10, "Problems: Decisions." Topic readings: Medicaid work requirements, healthcare, poverty in America.	
9	10/24	Stone, chapter 11, "Solutions: Inducements." Stone, chapter 12, "Solutions: Rules." Topic reading: Policing: Minneapolis report.	
10	10/31	One-on-one meetings on legislative reports.	One-on-one meetings with groups about legislative reports.
11	11/7	Election Day	One-on-one meetings with groups about legislative reports;legislative research reports due.
12	11/14	Stone, chapter 13, "Solutions: Facts." Topic readings: Immigration and public housing.	Discuss op-ed assignment; share example op-eds.
Thanksgiving Week	11/21		
13	11/28	Stone, chapter 14, "Solutions: Rights." Stone, chapter 15, "Solutions: Powers." Topic reading: Financial regulation	Op-eds due; discuss elevator pitch assignment.
14	12/5	Stone: "Conclusion and Policy Paradox in Action"	Elevator pitches/mock legislative meetings.

2. Planning

Include a timeline of deadlines and how you will complete your work. A few things to keep in mind:

- The format is up to you, but I encourage you to include something like an outline, calendar, or Gannt or other planning tool.
- Review the syllabus for upcoming deadlines, but also fill in how you will produce the component parts of those assignments. Take note of draft reviews in class as well.

[*Authors' Note: Some instructors prefer to set up group guidelines well before choosing a bill; others include bill choice as part of initial group meetings.*]

3. Bill Choice

Identify the bill you wish to support (or oppose) this term. Include the following:

- Title of the bill and bill number
- Link to the bill's text in the legislative database
- In approximately 100 words, summarize the bill. What problem is it trying to solve, and how does it address this problem?
- In approximately 150 words, describe *why* your group has chosen this bill. How does this bill engage your passions and interests? What makes this a good fit for your group? Why do you think you will be good advocates for it?

Proposals will be graded for content, clarity in writing, and responsiveness to these guidelines.

Sample Assignment Guidelines for Issue Brief

Each week, *identify an active issue in state and/or local politics.* This could be a bill pending before the legislature or city/town council, a local development deal, a protest or citizen event, or, really, any political phenomena of interest to you. The only requirement is that it should *not* be a federal/national political issue, but relevant to the *state or a locality* near us.

Then post a brief of *100–150 words* about the issue. The brief should be in *your* words, not the words of your source; *do not quote.*

Briefs have three components:

- A *summary* of the issue of concern. You should be able to explain what's going on (the conflict, question, or whatever) and the players involved.
- An *evaluation* or perspective on the issue. You might agree with one side or the other in a conflict, or point out the power dynamics involved.
- A *link* to a newspaper article, blog post, podcast, video, or other source for the issue.

Sample Student Submission for Issue Brief

The City of Richmond will rename a street, currently the Boulevard, to Arthur Ashe Boulevard. They are renaming it after the tennis star and civil rights activity Arthur Ashe. There was a lot of opposition to the bill from residents who worried about the cost and inconvenience, but the City Council voted overwhelmingly (8–0, with one abstention) to change the name.

I think this is an important change in Richmond's history that can help deal with the past. If the city let Confederate monuments stand around the corner on Monument Avenue for a century, then they should also commemorate the city's civil rights heroes and important African Americans.

(www.richmond.com/news/local/city-of-richmond/richmond-city-council-renames-boulevard-for-arthur-ashe/.)

NOTES

1. This literature is too voluminous to reference here, but there are many guides available online, particularly on the website of university teaching centers. See, for example, Indiana University Bloomington's Center for Innovative Teaching and Learning (https://citl.indiana.edu/teaching-resources/evidence-based/active-learning.html) and University of Minnesota's Center for Educational Innovation (https://cei.umn.edu/teaching-resources/active-learning/why-use-active-learning).

2. Probably the most widely circulated of these tools is the American Association of Colleges & Universities' VALUE rubric for teamwork, available at www.aacu.org/initiatives/value-initiative/value-rubrics/value-rubrics-teamwork.

3. See, for example, Eric Redman, *The Dance of Legislation: An Insider's Account of the Workings of the United States Senate* (Seattle: University of Washington Press, 2011).

4. "Projects and Resources," PBLWorks, accessed July 1, 2024, www.pblworks.org/resources-overview.

5. "ABLConnect," The Derek Bok Center for Teaching and Learning, Harvard University, accessed July 1, 2024, https://ablconnect.harvard.edu.

6. Penelope Muse Abernathy, *News Deserts and Ghost Newspapers: Will Local News Survive?* (Chapel Hill, NC: University of North Carolina Press, 2020).

7. See, for example, the Virginia Public Access Project's "VANews" daily newsletter at www.vpap.org/vanews.

8. Susan Clarke Schaar, *Your Guide to the Virginia General Assembly* (Richmond, VA: Virginia Senate Clerk's Office, n.d.).

9. *The 2023–2024 Guide to the Nevada Legislature* (Carson City, NV: Research Division, Nevada Legislative Counsel Bureau, 2023).

10. See, for example, the Legislative Reference Bureau of Hawaii's site at https://lrb.hawaii.gov/par/overview-of-the-legislative-process.

11. "Public Resources," ENACT, accessed July 1, 2024, www.enactnetwork.org/resources/view/public.

2
Building Relationships at Your State Legislature

THE LEGISLATURE in your home state likely has its own quirks and idiosyncrasies. Louis Brandeis famously called the states "laboratories of democracy," spaces where local government actors could experiment and innovate. But all that experimentation and innovation can result in bewildering differences from one state to another. Perhaps your students will be walking into a sprawling legislature with 424 members (New Hampshire) or a unicameral body of only 49 lawmakers (Nebraska). Perhaps the lawmakers with whom they are engaging are paid six-figure salaries (California), or maybe you're in New Mexico, where lawmakers receive no salary at all. Beyond this, the basic institutions of government, the procedures these legislatures follow, and even the political culture and professional etiquette can be radically unique.

Yet all state legislatures depend on *relationships*: to successfully complete their day-to-day business, to articulate issues to the public, to deliver for their constituents, to compromise and craft public policy. The most skilled and principled legislators will fail abysmally if they cannot build relationships with one another, with partisan and nonpartisan staff, with lobbyists and advocates, and with the broader public they have been elected to serve. The success or failure of a legislative session or a critical piece of legislation often hinges upon relationship building.

In the same way, successfully offering an ENACT course will depend upon *your* ability to build such relationships. The most enriching experiences in your class allow students to witness the actual operations of policymaking and to see the rhythm of lawmaking and advocacy in person. Here, again, individual states vary in their transparency and access. Some legislatures will cheerfully throw open the door and invite your students into the most intimate of policy settings. In other states, you'll be met by gatekeepers who want to curate, and even restrict access to, the experience.

Developing dense networks of professional relationships and institutional knowledge will be invaluable in helping your students access these settings. In addition, it will help them decipher what is happening in these spaces and partake in citizen advocacy themselves. When you build relationships with state policy experts who possess access and institutional knowledge, they can serve as a helpful guide for you and your students as you begin making sense of these fascinating (but often fast-paced and complex) environments.

Depending on your legislative context and your existing familiarity and relationships with those involved in state government, this process can seem a little daunting. Perhaps you have never engaged with state political decision-making yourself or you are relatively new to the state in which you're teaching. Or perhaps you are worried that lawmakers, staffers, and advocates navigating a busy legislative session simply will not have time or capacity to help you and your students gain knowledge and build new skills. These are reasonable concerns. But the successful development of ENACT courses across so many different state contexts suggests that they are not insurmountable.

Consider this example. In Maine, one of our ENACT fellows approached a state lawmaker with the bold idea of involving students in research-based advocacy around bills being debated in the ongoing legislative session. The faculty member knew this individual fairly well, but did so hesitantly, almost apologetically, assuming that involving students would be a burden for already busy lawmakers. Not so at all! "That would be great! We're often flying blind on a lot of these proposals and relying upon the testimony of professional lobbyists. This would fill an important gap," exclaimed the lawmaker. Obviously, we can't guarantee that every ENACT course will be received so enthusiastically right out of the gate. But we also should not assume that we know the needs and capacities of political settings in which we do not work on a day-to-day basis.

This chapter will equip you with the skills to successfully connect with individuals working for and within the state legislatures, who can help facilitate access to state policymaking and hands-on experiences for you and your students. We will present some important questions to consider when establishing connections and help you identify resources to assist you in making these connections. Whether you have consciously considered it or not, you likely already have a web of relationships that you can draw upon in initiating and building these relationships. We'll also consider strategies aimed at mitigating political risks associated with offering such a course and building support for such efforts internally within your institution. The chapter will close by presenting tangible resources such as email and phone scripts that you may rely upon as you take the all-important step of building relationships with lawmakers.

Key Questions

Where do you begin in connecting with state lawmakers or individuals with extensive professional experience in state legislatures?

Within grassroots political advocacy, political organizers will often involve citizen advocates at the outset of a campaign in a process called "power mapping." The purpose of this exercise is to help individuals think about the political leverage that they already potentially possess. Frequently, that power is *relational*. So, if we were to engage in this process, we would start to systematically map the webs of relationships we already have with lawmakers, advocacy organizations, and prominent community leaders—or those that we could build with relatively little effort. As an ENACT instructor, you can think about the relationships you would like to build or already have in a very similar way. (You can even build such power mapping into course activities for students; see the description of the stakeholder analysis assignment in chapter 3.)

As residents of communities, we are all constituents of elected representatives. In fact, by simply thinking about where we live and where we work, we can likely generate a list of our elected officials and those who represent the district in which our educational institutions reside (if you don't happen to live in the same district as your college or university). These connections should be even more apparent at the state level. Federal representatives are responsible for sizable districts, large staffs, and packed schedules. State legislators, on the other hand, can be much more accessible with fewer time constraints and gatekeepers. In some states, they might even be part-time elected officials, whose primary professional responsibility resides within your community: a local business owner, a teacher at your local school, a firefighter, a retiree looking to serve the public in their golden years, and so on.

These individuals represent *you* (or at least, that's their formal responsibility). So, you should feel empowered to reach out to these officials, explain what you are doing, and seek their assistance. Though our legislative leaders are elected to craft policy, most take constituent relations seriously and value the importance of educating the public and demystifying what happens in our state capitols. Beyond those currently holding office, you might also consider reaching out to former legislators, those who have retired or have recently lost contested elections. Though not currently in office, they can help guide you in how to connect with state policymakers and likely have a dense web of professional relationships to assist you and your students. Plus, they may have more time and capacity than a sitting legislator in the midst of a busy session.

However, if we go back to that hypothetical power-mapping exercise, your relationship as a constituent of a state legislator would only be the starting point. Perhaps you are involved with civic advocacy groups or volunteer organizations or are represented by a union. Many of these organizations will have staff or individuals who specialize in governmental relations and state policy advocacy. You can reach out to these individuals as well. You could potentially talk about the ways they might collaborate with your students: directing them to specific bills, translating what impacts legislation would have, etc. But such individuals also understand the state's web of political relationships. Working alongside such an advocate could be a great way to facilitate introductions and connections with lawmakers they trust and feel will be excited to connect with students. Many of our institutions of higher education have lobbyists and governmental relations professionals on staff. These individuals, too, can serve as valuable contacts when it comes to making connections.

Beyond lawmakers, what types of individuals can be useful in making connections at the state legislature?

For an engaging, experiential class focused on state policy, developing relationships with lawmakers is vital. But it need not be your starting point, and there might even be compelling reasons to prioritize other forms of relationship building as a means to setting up your course for long-term success.

For instance, there are currently sixteen states that place term limits on their state legislators.[1] Proponents argued for the necessity of such term limits to ensure turnover in our elected officials and prevent "career politicians" from growing distant from their constituents. Practically, however, this can mean that you cultivate a relationship with a lawmaker only to see them "termed out" and prevented from running again.

Even in states without term limits, elections happen, and incumbents may lose. In either case, you may end up building a relationship with a lawmaker only to see them leave office in the next election. Beyond electoral realities, in states with part-time, "citizen" legislatures, newly elected lawmakers may have limited practical policy experience before they take office, and in a first or even second term, they may still be learning about the fundamentals of policymaking themselves.

For these reasons, it's important to think about legislative relationship building not solely in terms of elected state representatives. Institutional knowledge does not reside in policymakers alone. They may not be—and frequently are *not*—the most knowledgeable individuals in the building. For a multitude of reasons, it may make sense to build connections with a variety of different types of professionals and policy actors.

So, what other types of actors might you seek to connect with? First and foremost, understanding the staffing landscape of your state legislature can be immensely helpful. Though staffing varies considerably from one state to another, every legislature will have some combination of partisan and nonpartisan staff.

- *Partisan staff.* Partisan staff work at the behest of legislative leadership for the minority and majority parties. In some states with full-time professional legislatures, the efforts of staff members might even be dedicated to a single lawmaker. These individuals typically have a range of responsibilities, including constituent services, research and policy development, drafting legislation and securing cosponsors, and public communications. Given their wide range of responsibilities, and the fact that their longevity in the position is not strictly tied to electoral outcomes or term limits, partisan staff can be an invaluable resource in understanding the granular details of state policymaking. Of course, you should remember that they are *partisan* staff, reflecting the interests of a particular political party that often reflects a particular ideology. So, in the interest of ensuring that students are exposed to multiple viewpoints, your goal would be to connect with multiple partisan staff from different political parties.

- *Nonpartisan staff.* In addition to partisan staff working on behalf of elected officials, all state legislatures will have some dedicated cohort of nonpartisan staff. These individuals do not serve at the pleasure of elected leadership or partisan officials and typically engage in more legalistic, analytical, and financial roles within state policymaking. For instance, a nonpartisan staffer's job may entail translating a general idea for a legislative bill into the appropriate legal language (often called the "revisor's office"). Other nonpartisan legislative analysts may staff committees, responding to technical questions about specific pieces of legislation or being accountable for entire policy areas. Legislative research staff may be on hand to address questions and inquiries from individual lawmakers. Nonpartisan staff may explore the financial implications of proposed legislation, investigating whether it would impose costs, generate revenue for the state, or be "revenue neutral."

  These are highly technical but incredibly important staff positions. Such staffers can be tremendously helpful to you, particularly as your students try to make sense of complex legislation or aim to understand the legislative history that has led to a present proposal. Also helpfully, turnover within these positions tends to be less frequent than in partisan positions or elected office. Furthermore, nonpartisan positions can present your students with a more holistic view of the institutions of government, and one less influenced by partisanship.

- *Policy advocates and lobbyists.* We often think of "lobbyist" as a dirty word, likely due to stereotypes of high-priced, unscrupulous Washington, DC, operatives doing the bidding of any cause or organization willing to pay their exorbitant fees. This rarely captures what we see at the state level, and arguably doesn't even do justice to the realities of the national policy landscape. During a state legislative session, on any given day at the statehouse, a range of individuals will be engaged in legislative advocacy, working to support or oppose policy, to secure state funding, and to represent their own interests or those of organizations that they represent.

Of course, not all who engage in advocacy are considered lobbyists. Our ENACT students are not lobbyists, nor are many of the individuals they will encounter over the course of the class who aim to influence legislation (lawmakers, grassroots citizen advocates, staff, etc.). The definition of lobbying varies from state to state but will typically involve both receiving compensation for the work one does on behalf of an organization or interest group and reaching a certain threshold of activity (usually a certain number of hours devoted to advocacy within a thirty-day period). Lobbyists typically have to identify as such while in the statehouse and can run the gamut from representing gigantic corporations like Walmart and Apple to locally based, grassroots civic organizations working on issues specific to your state.

Those who have experience in engaging in legislative advocacy or who do such work professionally are also a helpful resource as you begin to develop your ENACT course. As with staffers, they are not subject to the whims of the electorate or term limits. So, lobbyists can have lengthy professional experience that some state lawmakers may lack; many may have previously held staff positions or served in the legislature. Beyond their background, their work is often specialized to specific issue areas, whereas policymakers must consider a wide range of issues. If your course has a particular focus or topic area, finding the relevant policy advocate who has a history of policy engagement and advocacy at the state level can unlock policy-relevant information and an acute understanding of the history leading up to contemporary debates. In addition, the impact of a lobbyist or citizen advocate depends upon their reputation and their web of relationships with those who hold power. Thus, these individuals can be helpful in directing you to staffers and lawmakers with whom you may work.

- *Political journalists.* Most states will have at least a few journalists, perhaps several, whose job includes covering state politics. They may be working full time on the statehouse beat, split between legislative politics and other topic areas, or part of an increasing corps of reporters employed by nonprofit news organizations.[2] Particularly if this individual is a veteran reporter, they will have a fascinating and rich set of insights to convey to your students about state politics. Yet beyond making the dynamics of the statehouse come alive, they will be able to contextualize debates and deliberation over legislation occurring over multiple sessions. They will be able to situate the individual initiatives being considered in relation to the past legislative leadership's goals; relevant policy organizations and political interests within the state; and dynamics among state governors, legislators, and the perspectives of constituents and the general public. As with lobbyists and advocates, success as a political journalist requires maintaining a web of professional relationships and developing a reputation for being fair, trustworthy, and thoughtful. Thus, political journalists (in addition to being valuable resources in their own right) likely know who within state politics can be a potential collaborator on your course.

This is not an exhaustive list of the types of individuals you might connect with in order to successfully plan and execute an ENACT course on state policymaking, but it is a start. In addition, the specifics will likely vary from state to state. In a small, densely networked state like Vermont or New Hampshire, it may be feasible to reach out to individuals within all the categories above. In larger states such as California or New York, with a more professionalized and complex policy landscape, this may be beyond your capacity.

Whatever the context, what you will likely find is that individuals in one or more of the categories above are excited at the prospect of your class, eager to know more, and want to collaborate on educating your students about the complex realities of your state's political and policy landscape, a professional realm to which they have dedicated their lives and careers.

Frequently, in teaching this course, lawmakers and staffers note the absence of young people engaged in the meaningful work of state government, whether that be citizen advocacy before the legislature or entering into some of the roles they've inhabited for their entire careers. Many students care deeply about the issues they're considering but might lack knowledge about the process and institutions necessary to engage. Your work can help build this "pipeline" of engagement.

It was exhilarating to sit down with the senator to discuss the bill and the impact it would have on Massachusetts families—using examples of people I knew whose lives would be changed by the passage of it. Suddenly, the ideas of lobbying and legislating felt tangible and accessible to me. Advocacy wasn't just men in suits speed walking through the halls of Congress. It was also the experience of sitting down with a local official and sharing stories from my community.

ELAINA PEVIDE, Brandeis University

In what other ways can your institution support this work?

We may think of our educational institutions as apolitical settings in which learning happens, but colleges and universities are also political actors. They seek resources, cultivate carefully crafted public reputations, and must be mindful of public policy developments that would support or hinder their organizational missions. For instance, the fate of public state colleges and universities, as well as community colleges, can critically hinge on decisions about appropriations in the state legislature. Private institutions may be less *directly* financially beholden to state legislatures but are likely to encounter a slew of legislation each session that impacts their day-to-day operations: labor laws, public health policies, participation in professional certification and licensure training, and so much more. At the very least, representatives of our institutions want elected officials to be aware of the educational and outreach work they do, to see its value, and not view institutional efforts with skepticism or hostility. Ideally, they seek to recruit lawmakers and elected officials as enthusiastic advocates for their work.

Thus, there may be staff at your university who can help facilitate connections to policymakers with whom the university already has relationships. In addition, there are likely alumni of your university who serve in state elected office, have done so in the past, or have pursued a non-elected, policy-relevant career such as those listed above. Beyond alumni, there might even be instructors, researchers, or staff at the institution who are present or past state officeholders. Given their knowledge of both your educational institution and the dynamics of your state's legislature, these individuals can be an excellent resource, and their proximity on campus makes their in-person involvement less logistically challenging than engaging individuals off-campus.

What kinds of planning and logistics should you consider to develop effective relationships?

The suggestions above primarily concern *making connections* with lawmakers and those with expertise in state politics and your state legislature. Of course, this is only the first step in relationship building. Equally important is cultivating and sustaining those relationships over time. Below, we consider both how to make initial contact with important collaborators along with how to reach these longer-term goals.

As with any engaged course, you'll want to start your planning and outreach efforts well in advance of the initial offering of the course. This is particularly important if you're not already well-versed in your state's legislative politics and political system as a whole. It may take time to connect with the different individuals listed above and their appetite and capacity for collaboration, as well as to get a sense of what level of direct legislative engagement will be possible or appropriate in your state.

In a similar vein, knowing when and how to reach out will likely depend on the rhythm of your state's legislative session. The state-to-state variation, enshrined in our federalist system of governance mentioned at the outset of this chapter, likely means that this is a bit different in each state. Those with experience in state legislative politics can tell you when lawmakers and other staffers might have the most capacity to meet with you and thoughtfully consider ways they might play a role in your course, as well as times of the year in which all parties involved are overwhelmed and emails and phone calls may go unanswered. An added consideration for elected officials, of course, is the campaign cycle. In addition to their work within the legislature, they must concern themselves with getting reelected, a cumbersome process that will likely involve fundraising, connecting directly with voters, and participating in the broader work of the party they represent in a busy election year (campaign events, caucuses, conventions, etc.). Thus, success in this endeavor requires not only knowing who to talk to, but also *when* they'll have the capacity to talk to you.

Like any relationship, your attempts to connect with those involved in state legislative politics may result in dead ends. You might reach out by email or phone multiple times and not receive any response, or those you contact might direct you toward others. There might be significant delays as you wait to hear back. In such cases, it's entirely appropriate to follow up or nudge these individuals. In our experience teaching these classes, legislators particularly are thankful for follow-ups and reminders. Their inbox or voicemail often involves a process of "triage," where they're responding to absolutely critical messages and requests and, inevitably, some folks fall through the cracks. Such difficulties in making connections are not about you or the value of the work you're doing. They simply speak to how extraordinarily busy many of those involved with state legislative politics are.

Persistence tends to pay off in establishing these relationships. However, at a certain point, you may want to simply move on and shift your outreach to someone else. You may end up reconnecting at some point in the future, but if someone is struggling to return your call or answer an email, the time may not be right.

When you do establish contact with a potential collaborator, it's important to clearly articulate what you are asking them to do: help orient students to the state legislature, visit the class for a guest session on state political journalism, work with students to help decipher the language of state legislation, and so on. Training in political advocacy and organizing often focuses on the importance of a strong, clear "ask," and this form of relationship building is no different. It is also important to be strategic in what you are asking these individuals to do. In the ENACT courses taught across the country, the participation of different legislative participants varies from those who effectively function as "co-teachers" to one-off Q&A sessions conducted via Zoom to occasional behind-the-scenes support in preparation of the course. If you're initiating a new relationship, you might start with a relatively small request, build rapport, and then gauge the individual's willingness and capacity to be more deeply engaged in your course.

Similarly, you should be clear in presenting what the students can provide. This will vary based on how you structure your course and what you are actually asking the students to do. It might simply be that you are getting students excited and engaged in state legislative politics and potentially building out that "pipeline" of future lawmakers, political journalists, and policy professionals mentioned earlier in this chapter. People serving in these capacities are likely passionate about their roles and excited to share their wisdom and insights with others, especially if it might make a formative impact on their eventual professional trajectories.

But sometimes the payoff is more immediate. For lawmakers, students may play a role in policy development, identifying an issue in need of action and proposing a policy solution to help address the issue. Your students may end up engaged in legislative testimony, providing evidence-based, thoughtful insights on the direction the legislature should take before the relevant committee. Students might become mobilized around the issues they're researching and advocate at different stages in the policy process: to connect with other lawmakers prior to a floor vote, to advocate for funding during the appropriations process, to call upon the governor to pass a bill or lawmakers to override a veto, and more. As noted above, students can be highly effective messengers on a variety of issues and inject insight and lived experience into the policy process that too often is lacking.

Perhaps the most important aspect of cultivating and sustaining a relationship with legislative partners is gratitude for the individual's time and effort. This is particularly the case for more demanding forms of collaboration in which an individual is taking significant time and energy to play an educational role, orienting students toward your state's legislative politics. Such instances are also a good opportunity to amplify this individual's efforts through the community outreach and public relations outlets available on your campus: your news division, departmental and institutional social media accounts, etc. At the state level, many lawmakers effectively have to function as their own social media managers. Amplifying their public outreach with students (with their permission, of course) might be seen as advantageous to them.

However, you don't have to see such outreach as promoting a specific official; it can also help broaden public understanding of their role and the valuable work they do on behalf of the public, often with demanding responsibilities and relatively little pay. Constituents often only contact their lawmakers when they are upset or dissatisfied: they're demanding they vote a certain way, or they're upset about a certain outcome, or they're engaging with constituent services because some state agency has wronged them. Promotional work such as this helps remind the public of the ways that lawmakers are often driven by a sense of public service and self-sacrifice and aim to do right by their constituents and help build the next generation of leaders.

Assignments and Other Key Course Components

Contacting Potential Collaborators

You will likely first reach out to potential collaborators through an introductory email. Brevity and directness are key in this initial outreach. The individuals with whom you're hoping to connect are likely quite busy, so your initial contact should be brief and to the point. If you send a sprawling, multi-paragraph email that tries to present a comprehensive overview of the course and who you are, your contact likely won't have the capacity to read it (or at least, not closely). Remember that the objective here is simply to introduce yourself, explain the course, and explore possibilities of collaboration. Relationship building is an iterative process; hopefully, there will be time for more meaningful engagement and relationship building later. Finally, note that, in our experience with legislators and staff, persistence pays off. You may need to pursue multiple attempts at outreach before you're able to connect with the individual or organization you're contacting or someone adjacent to them.

Later in this chapter we offer sample templates for email and phone/ Zoom scripts that you might use in reaching out to potential collaborators. These are meant to be a general guide for outreach, and you should feel free to deviate from such a script to personalize your message, taking into account the characteristics of your state and those you are contacting.

> *The class made me a more effective speaker, writer, and lobby[ist], and gave me the confidence to bring issues that I care about to local, state, and federal representatives.*
>
> —from a survey of Brandeis alumni who participated in ENACT course

Additional Resources

Morgan Carroll's *Take Back Your Government: A Citizen's Guide to Grassroots Change*[3]

This citizen's guide, written by a former Colorado statehouse representative and state senator, is a valuable resource for thinking about all stages of grassroots citizen advocacy. Carroll uses her expertise to lay out how to navigate the landscape of state legislative politics as well as offering resources for all stages of grassroots citizen advocacy. This volume can be helpful in your initial planning and relationship building, but also offers resources (and specific examples to follow) for all stages of the advocacy process.

National Conference of State Legislatures (NCSL) Legislative Calendar Guide[4]

The National Conference of State Legislatures (NCSL) is an extraordinary resource for those teaching ENACT courses. One of the many helpful tools you can access is a guide to state legislative calendars. So, as you consider the timing of your outreach to legislators, staffers, and those involved in state legislative politics, this can be a useful guide. Your state legislature will typically have this information on its website as well. Keep in mind that legislatures may be called into "a special session" outside of the typical calendar, or extraordinary circumstances may require them to extend a session as they race to wrap up their legislative business.

National Conference of State Legislatures (NSCL) "Working with Legislators" Handbook[5]

Another great resource from NCSL is their handbook for working with legislators. Though ostensibly aimed at criminal justice stakeholders engaged in advocacy, it provides good general information about the landscape of state politics. Information is provided for all fifty states, so regardless of where you are working to develop your course, NCSL can help you sort out the basic institutional features of your state and offers good advice for thinking about how to effectively establish connections and engage with lawmakers.

Conclusion

Hopefully, this chapter has taken what seems to be a daunting and possibly even overwhelming task and brought it down to earth a bit. One thing you should keep in mind is that state legislators are typically ordinary people with an inclination to serve the public. While their primary responsibility is deliberation and making the law, serving their constituents can take a variety of forms. Many such lawmakers will be excited at the prospect of educating students about how this process actually works as well as potentially serving as a catalyst that will inspire a student to think about professional trajectories in state government. While our state legislators are often tasked with an extraordinary set of responsibilities, the success of ENACT courses nationally demonstrates the ways that many still make time to help orient students toward state legislative politics and find this process personally and professionally rewarding.

In addition, it's hopefully clear that there are many paths to making such connections, as there is an array of different individuals whose professional orbit revolves around state legislative politics. In fact, there may be strategic reasons to put your primary effort into building relationships with those parallel to lawmakers, such as staffers, policy advocates, representatives of civic organizations, and political journalists. It is these individuals whose professional fates are not subject to the shifting winds of elections or the concrete realities of term limits.

Formation of such relationships hinges upon clarity in communication, being persistent while also expressing gratitude, and extending grace and understanding. Furthermore, ENACT courses offer a way to lift up and amplify the good, public-facing work being done by our legislators in ways that can sustain existing relationships and open the door to new forms of cooperation.

Sample Email Script for Potential Collaborator

Dear ____________,

I hope you are well. My name is ____________ and I am a [*title*] at [*institution*].

[*Authors' Note: If you have a connection to the person you're contacting or were referred by an intermediary, mention this here. Say something about how and why you're reaching out to them specifically.*]

I'm reaching out because I'm in the process of developing a course that will introduce students to the state legislative process. Many of our students care deeply about or are directly impacted by state policy, and the goal of this course is to foster greater civic engagement with our state legislature.

I'm hoping that I could set up a time to talk to you more about how you might engage with the students and help orient them to the important work that you do for your constituents and our state.

Could we set up a time to meet or chat via Zoom/phone so that I can tell you more about this initiative?

[*Authors' Note: Conclude with some logistical information regarding availability and how to meet.*]

Thanks very much!

Sample Phone/Zoom Script for Potential Collaborator

Hello! Thank you for making the time to chat with me today.

[*Authors' Note: Briefly introduce yourself and talk about how you became interested in state politics.*]

I'm reaching out because I'm in the process of planning an exciting course that will educate students about the state legislative process and help equip them with the tools to be more engaged and knowledgeable citizens.

Students care deeply about and are personally impacted by policy issues, but may not understand the ways they can be involved in the process. Since 2016, a national network called ENACT has helped train college faculty to teach these types of engaged courses all over the United States. I'm hoping to offer such a course here in our state.

Students in these courses choose pieces of legislation before their state legislature on topics they care about deeply. I guide them to research the policy issues, its history and implications, and the unique characteristics of our state politics and institutions. The goal is to demystify state politics and help students engage directly in ways that are respectful, evidence-based, and help enrich the policy process.

[*Authors' Note: Here is where you can add your "ask"; what are you asking this potential collaborator to do?*]

I'd be happy to talk more about the course or answer any questions you might have.

[*Authors' Note: From here, hopefully the interaction becomes more conversational. You should come prepared to ask questions about timing, the types of students who will be involved, how much time and energy this will demand of your potential collaborator, and the potential direct or indirect benefits to them.*]

NOTES

1. "The Term-Limited States," National Conference of State Legislatures, last modified August 3, 2023, www.ncsl.org/about-state-legislatures/the-term-limited-states.

2. Naomi Forman-Katz, Elisa Shearer, and Katerina Eva Matsa, "Nonprofit News Outlets Are Playing a Growing Role in Statehouse Coverage," Pew Research Center, April 29, 2022, www.pewresearch.org/short-reads/2022/04/29/nonprofit-news-outlets-are-playing-a-growing-role-in-statehouse-coverage.

3. Morgan Carroll, *Take Back Your Government: A Citizen's Guide to Grassroots Change* (Chicago: Fulcrum, 2012).

4. "2024 State Legislative Session Calendar," National Conference of State Legislatures, last modified July 8, 2024, www.ncsl.org/about-state-legislatures/2024-state-legislative-session-calendar.

5. *State Legislators: Who They Are and How to Work with Them* (Washington, DC: National Conference of State Legislators, 2018).

3
Legislative Research

Americans love the idea of term limits. A 2023 polling report from the Pew Research Center[1] suggested that almost nine in ten Americans would prefer to limit the number of terms for members of Congress. Similar results have been reported at the state level; as noted earlier, sixteen states currently have some form of term limit for state legislators. And yet results are mixed. Political scientists argue that rather than increasing responsiveness to constituents, term limits instead empower unelected officials, especially staffers and lobbyists.[2]

The truth is that often overwhelmed legislators desperately rely on expertise from these unelected contributors to the legislative process. These can be trusted staffers and academic experts, but also the skilled advocates who know a subject area and can explain complicated policy issues. Sometimes these advocates are highly paid lobbyists representing a specific interest or industry. But sometimes they are citizen advocates—people with a passion or interest in a policy issue and a desire for reform and policy change. An advocate armed with some basic research and familiarity with a policy issue can often be welcomed by a concerned legislator, as well as encourage the legislator to make important changes by passing a bill.

Therefore, a key component of the ENACT course model is research. This should not be surprising—developing content knowledge and research skills are key goals of almost any college experience, and cornerstones of higher education. In fact, the research component of ENACT courses can often be the one with which teachers new to the model are most comfortable just because of this overlap with other experiences. ENACT research assignments are very similar to a "regular" class paper or presentation, and both teachers and students new to active learning might be able to find their footing in such a traditional classroom experience.

This chapter covers the legislative research component of the ENACT model, with particular emphasis on two aspects. First, students need to identify a bill for which they want to advocate. This may be harder than it sounds; both students and instructors need to consider a number of factors, including the political environment, student demographics, and feasibility. Since ENACT places students in an active legislative milieu, instructors need to guide students in bill choice, planning, and scheduling; they must also consider contingency plans in case events overtake their students' legislative agenda. Second, once students identify a bill for which they want to advocate, they should become mini experts in the bill's policy milieu. They do not need to know everything, of course, but they should have available some basic data concerning the policy problem at hand; familiarity with arguments both for and against the proposed legislation; and a clear case, including some helpful narratives, for why the bill is the best possible solution to the problem.

Key Questions

What are the cultural and political contexts surrounding your state legislature?

You don't have to be a political scientist to know that states vary widely in their culture; Mississippi and Alaska are very different in their climate, for sure, but also their norms, rules, and practices, in everything from sayings and accents to clothing and popular flavors. But ever since Daniel Elazar's famous study,[3] political scientists have noted the differences in *political* culture among different regions and states. The norms and practices of political institutions vary just as widely as the type of barbecue or name for soda.

State legislatures are certainly not excluded from this analysis, and being familiar with the style and practice of legislating in your own state can be very helpful. Interactions with legislators can be easier if you know what "bumping" a bill means,[4] or if you understand why "crossover" is such an important deadline.[5] But while you can probably succeed without knowing the exact lingo of your legislature, there are some particular aspects of legislatures with which you really should familiarize yourself and that are essential to success in an ENACT course.

First, understanding the ideological and partisan makeup of the broader state culture, and the legislature in particular, will help you and your students understand what kinds of bills are likely to be considered. Reproductive rights legislation may fall on deaf ears in a legislature dominated by pro-life conservatives. Infrastructure bills may be highly controversial in a state with a long history of regional conflict over highway and transit development. A seemingly innocuous or technical public school reform might become part of a cultural battle among partisan officials over the future of education.

The obvious thing to know is the partisan control of the state. Is there a Democratic or Republican "trifecta" that has control of both houses and the governor's office? Is party control split, either between the legislature's houses or between the legislative and executive branches? Is there a history of bipartisan cooperation on any issue area? Or has polarization led to gridlock or, alternatively, one party's domination? Partisanship is often a key indicator of ideological lean, but it's not always determinative. How "conservative" are the Republicans, and how "progressive" are the Democrats?

If you are unsure of the answers to these questions, there are places you can go to find out. Being well-versed in local news coverage can help guide you. That is, it can help *if* such coverage exists; another challenge in today's political environment in some states is the lack of local news coverage in a number of areas. As local newspapers especially struggle and "news deserts" proliferate, trying to find alternative sources of information can be essential. A number of states feature local "bloggers" using whatever the latest social media platform and/or subscription model is prominent, as well as citizen activists who chronicle public meetings and events. As noted above, your faculty colleagues, in the political science department and elsewhere, may be well-versed in the state's political structures and may act as guides to the legislature. Using your institution's alumni network or other connections to find "plugged-in" experts as advisors can be useful—state officials and staffers, government relations professionals, and nonprofit organizations with advocacy efforts can let you know what's going on behind the scenes, as well as serve as informative guest speakers for your students.

At the same time, it helps to remember that state legislators are open and accountable to their constituents. All state legislatures have a mandate to be open and accessible to public input; in the experience of ENACT fellows and teachers, most individual legislators fully support and even embrace this mandate. Legislators and their staff are typically welcoming and accepting of all input, even if they might ask challenging questions and raise concerns about particular bills. (In fact, those kinds of challenges and concerns should be encouraging, as they signal sincere engagement and interest on their part.)

The one exception to this encouraging story is an important one for faculty to remember and occurs outside the context of individual meetings. Higher education has more and more become an arena for political and cultural battles to be waged, particularly when public institutions (and tax dollars) are involved. Legislators in some states are challenging curriculum, institutional priorities, and funding through budgeting, political appointments, legislating, and rhetoric. Individual faculty can sometimes become targets of these kinds of bad-faith political challenges. Depending on the political environment in your state, the ENACT model may open up faculty and students to criticism, public protest, even harassment. Contingent and early-career faculty without tenure are most vulnerable to these kinds of attacks.

Still, there is risk to any active learning experience that ventures outside of the classroom, and a culture of fear in the academy does a disservice to our students. You can and should make yourself aware of the policies and supports in place at your institution to protect both their students and themselves. Guidance from institutional leadership, college and university counsel, and faculty advocacy groups such as the American Association of University Professors (AAUP) can support you as you engage in this and similar work. You can insulate yourself through class structure as well, by staying clearly and explicitly nonpartisan or bipartisan in the choice of mentors or advisors, guest speakers, and other participants. Keeping records of bipartisan outreach to legislators and staffers may help defuse any possible accusations of bias if that remains a concern in your state.

What kinds of bills/issues should your students choose?

The choice of bill is obviously an important decision, for both the instructor and the students. Just in terms of course mechanics, instructors can choose from a wide array of possibilities. Still, most ENACT instructors separate students into groups, with each group identifying a single unique bill on which they will focus their advocacy efforts. It is certainly possible for students to identify multiple bills, particularly if they are all related to a single issue; indeed, advocacy coalitions sometimes identify a broad legislative agenda even for a single legislative session. Still, instructors should be wary of overcomplicating the ENACT experience for students, especially if they are incorporating ENACT elements into an existing course. A single bill provides focus to student advocacy efforts—and instructor management.

Conversely, an entire class could work on a single issue or bill. This may work best if tackling a related legislative agenda, with different student groups working on bills that are related. If all students are working on the same bill, instructors and students should consider how best to manage advocacy to avoid duplicative effort, while also enabling all students to engage in the full ENACT experience. Will you assign student teams to different legislative offices? If some students work on developing advocacy materials for legislators, while others focus on media campaigns, do any of them miss out on aspects of the advocacy process? Having each student group take "ownership" of their own bill suggests the simplest approach, but as with everything ENACT, instructors should consider their own comfort and course learning objectives.

Instructors certainly could identify bills they think are appropriate and assign them to students. Still, principles of active learning, particularly those concerning project-based learning, suggest that students learn more, and more effectively, if they have some ownership over their work.[6] Instructors can instead carefully constrain student choices to ensure that they have a successful ENACT experience. Constraints might be best considered through a matrix aligning along two axes, as depicted in figure 3.1: internal vs. external factors, and interest vs. perception.

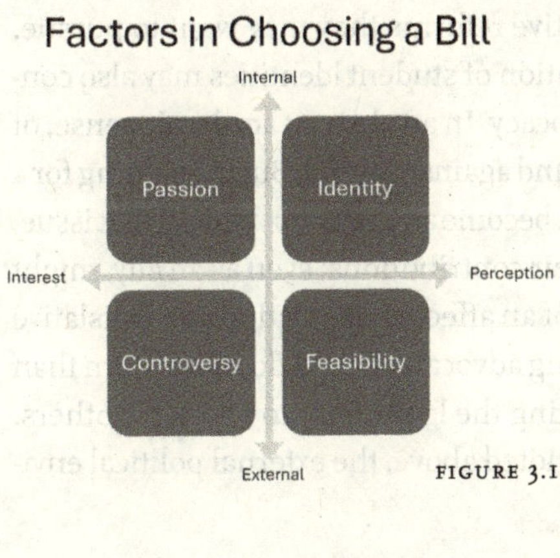

FIGURE 3.1. Bill Selection Matrix.

Through this matrix, we can identify four related factors that can influence the choice of a bill for advocacy.

- *Internal-Interest: Passion.* Ideally, the bill that students choose connects in some way to their interests, concerns, and experiences—what are often described as a student's *passions*. Some interests might be obviously tailored for political work and, therefore, bill choice; a student might describe themselves as an environmentalist, for example, or have a long history of volunteering for animal shelters. Others may have clear hobbies or interests, such as hunting or athletics.

  In-class exercises and reflection assignments can be used early in the course to help students articulate these passions, which can then be translated into keywords for searches of legislatives databases or conversations with legislators and staff about pending bills. When students work in groups, as the ENACT model strongly suggests, aligning student passions can be challenging. Still, you might steer students toward shared experiences and interests. For example, if students are all recent high school graduates, their shared experiences in K–12 education might connect them to particular education bills. You can even guide, encourage, or dictate group assignments based on shared passions as well.
- *Internal-Perception: Identity.* You and your students should carefully consider how their identities connect and contribute to their ENACT advocacy. From an internal perspective, identity broadly informs the passions and interests that students may bring to the class. A student may draw on their cultural background and history, ethnicity and/or race, gender and sexuality, and the experiences that may have been shaped by many such factors to consider which legislative reforms they may want to pursue.

  The perception and interpretation of student identities may also contribute to the success of their advocacy. In an abstract academic sense, of course any student may argue for and against any bill. But in standing for a bill's issue, students in some sense become an avatar for a side of that issue, and they should consider how their contributions, even as an ally, might be interpreted by both members of an affected population and legislative actors. Even the most well-meaning advocates might do more harm than good if they are perceived as lacking the legitimacy to speak for others.
- *External-Interest: Controversy.* As noted above, the external political envi-

ronment can offer challenges to instructors and students. And while any serious effort of engaging in politics might entail picking a fight, you and your students might consider how much of a fight you're willing to pick. Students can learn a lot about politics and the legislature when engaging with hotly contested issues; still, the risks noted above may interfere with the course's learning objectives, as well as have a host of unintended consequences for the instructor and institution.

One approach taken by some ENACT instructors is to encourage students to seek out procedural or institutional reforms; "good governance" advocacy can sometimes be more easily perceived by external actors as nonpartisan and nonideological. Still, even procedural matters like voting windows and ballot access have more recently been viewed by some through a partisan lens. It can help to emphasize the importance of civic discourse throughout the process, while encouraging students to acknowledge the concerns and arguments of opponents to their bill. If you stay "plugged in" to what's going on in your particular legislature, you can help students navigate these tricky waters.

- *External-Perception: Feasibility*. As noted often in this volume, students should not be evaluated on whether a bill passes; it would be cruel to give students a grade based on the whims of legislators. Still, part of the excitement of participating in an ENACT class—and, really, all forms of project-based learning—is that the stakes are real. Your chosen bill might become a law, and you can play a role in making an important change in your state. This sense of stakes can be dramatically lessened if there's a consensus in the political environment that the student's chosen bill is dead on arrival.

  Again, noting the role of student choice, their passionate engagement with an issue may drive their choice of bill to the point that they are unconcerned about the chances of passage. On the other hand, any bill, even a noncontroversial one, may be killed in committee or fail a floor vote for a host of reasons. You should prepare students for the possibility of a bill's failure, as well as offer opportunities for students to reflect on the importance of advocacy even in the face of effective opposition. (See below.)

Finally, one thing that you and your students should always remember—again, as with any project-based learning experience that engages with life outside the classroom—is that the bills chosen by students, if passed, may have real consequences for any affected individuals and communities. Both instructors and students should carefully consider the risks of harm to any vulnerable populations.

How much research is necessary?

Your students may be apprehensive about the level of expertise needed to be a successful advocate. Students particularly may feel anxiety about meeting with legislators, where they might be "exposed" as lacking necessary knowledge and expertise. They might imagine busy, stern, and brusque adults (in suits, of course) wondering why these kids are wasting their time. Of course, most advocacy experiences involve nothing of the sort—not least of which is that many legislative staffers are recent college graduates, barely older than the student advocates.

Student anxieties can be managed through a variety of early-course experiences, including an "orientation" visit, or a shadow day following other advocates on legislative visits. Still, even if anxiety about the actual meeting is lessened, there may remain concerns about how much knowledge is necessary to be the expert in the room. Certainly, students could spend the entire semester studying the bill and related issues surrounding it. But the ENACT experience aims to immerse students in the advocacy experience, and sooner rather than later.

You might remind students that it does not take much knowledge about a bill to develop much more expertise than most. Particularly in part-time legislatures, even the most well-educated officials and staffers have difficulty staying on top of all of the various bills introduced in a session. Again, advocates often play a valuable role in informing legislators of what a bill actually aims to accomplish, as well as the various arguments and data for and against those aims. Almost all legislative offices welcome input, but ENACT participants should remember that this input is helpful more often than not.

If you are unclear about the level of expertise necessary, you could arrange for a mock visit with an advisor (such as a sitting or former legislator or staffer) or even an early "trial" day with some friendly offices. Students can practice their meeting conversations in a welcoming environment and get specific feedback on holes in their knowledge or particular questions they might want to address; legislators often care deeply about fiscal impact, for example, or they may want to hear more about the opposing side's arguments. Even if there are no practice meetings, students should evaluate their first few meetings to see whether they are getting similar questions or concerns from participants and engage in further research accordingly.

The number one rule of advocacy that government relations professionals often espouse is that you must above all *be honest*. Students should not pretend to know something they do not or promise something they cannot deliver. You can encourage students to admit when they are unsure or do not know the answer to a question, and even have them practice doing so. They should know that it is perfectly fine to do so! Students should just let the questioner know that they will find out the answer to the question, and then they should follow through on that promise to provide it after the meeting.

Finally, it helps students if you are familiar with the resources necessary to support the particular kind of knowledge to develop expertise in a bill. Academics are likely to be accomplished researchers, but your own expertise may be limited to the sources of knowledge for your own discipline—books, archives, peer-reviewed journals, etc. Certainly, the skills and norms of academic research often apply to any kind of research project—identifying relevant data, properly citing sources, and avoiding plagiarism are important here as well. Still, policy research may require different resources. It can help if instructors know of the relevant news sources for a particular state or region. Students may also need to dig into policy research and data produced by think tanks, nonprofit groups, and government agencies. You may wish to call on legislative advisors or coalition partners about where to find data and arguments, but also campus resources like library staff.

> *I met with individuals from [advocacy groups]. . . . These professionals from the Des Moines community provided me with insight I could not find in research. They were blunt. They were honest. They were inquisitive. But most of all, they were supportive. . . . Now, I am more determined than ever to lobby for this bill this legislative season. . . . This would not have been possible without the class . . . and our community interactions with leaders and advocates from around Des Moines.*
>
> Taylor Weigel, Drake University, Iowa

Should your students find bills to support or oppose?

One thing to keep in mind is that legislative advocacy is just as often about opposing "bad" bills as supporting "good" ones. Many advocacy coalitions spend much of their time attempting to stop legislation that would, for example, change regulation to add new constraints or remove existing ones. To use one example from a policy area that should be familiar to faculty, higher education advocates sometimes speak up to oppose efforts to impose curriculum requirements on state university systems, such as a required way to teach history.

Still, students may find the ENACT experience more positive if they are working on a reform rather than trying to block bad or misinformed actors. One underlying goal of the ENACT experience is to get students excited and empowered about political change. Fighting a type of "rearguard" action might run the danger of leading them to be much more cynical about politics. Again, your own comfort level with the legislative process can matter here, as well as the particular passions and interests of your students and the political environment in your state.

What if a chosen bill becomes inactive?

As noted above, the feasibility of your students' advocacy project should matter to you from the beginning; while students' passions and interests are important, you might do students a disservice by helping them down an advocacy path of "certain death." You will greatly assist your students if you take care to understand the legislative process and calendar, as well as the direction in which the political winds are blowing. Still, no matter how carefully you plan, you are engaging with a live legislative process. At any point, a student bill may fail a floor vote, be continued to another session, or be killed in committee. Instructors should have at least some strategies in place to accommodate such events in the legislature.

One possibility upon bill failure is to ask students to pivot to a different bill. Sometimes this can be simple, as multiple legislators may be approaching the same problem; indeed, a bill can often be consolidated into, or give way for, a similar effort from a colleague. Even a bill that takes a different approach to the same issue might allow for a fairly smooth shift in student advocacy, with much of the same research and arguments applying to a new bill.

On the other hand, choosing a completely new bill with a different topic presents some challenges for the ENACT model, as students may have to scramble to research and develop arguments for the new issue under the time constraints of class; nor may it be fair to ask certain students to duplicate classwork due to circumstances beyond their control. You should carefully consider how best to balance class constraints of time management, fairness, and feasibility with the desire to provide opportunities for students to fully engage in the advocacy process.

A different approach involves acknowledging the failure of the bill, and then asking students to discover alternative paths for advocacy. Challenging students to consider next steps beyond the current legislative session may be one way to enhance the class's learning, especially if the challenged group shares their insights with the rest of the class. You could ask students to generate a political map of legislators who voted for and against their bill and design strategies for producing a different outcome in the future. If their bill dies before they get a chance to participate in legislative visits, students could still attend committee hearings on issues related to their bill or meet with friendly legislators to debrief what happened. You might ask other student groups to invite the affected students along as observers to their own meetings. Finally, as noted later in this volume, reflection and other culminating assignments offer an important opportunity to process the legislative experience, as well as identify lessons learned from any bill outcome.

Assignments and Other Key Course Components

Legislative Research Report

Student passion and interest in a bill may not be matched by expertise in its policy arena. In order to provide the scaffolding for students to develop the necessary expertise in their chosen bill's content area, a research assignment can be helpful and probably even essential. This assignment often takes the form of a written research report, sometimes accompanied by an in-class presentation, assigned shortly after the choice of bill.

As hinted above, instructors who are new to active learning experiences may find this assignment to be the easiest to implement in the ENACT class. Research papers and presentations are a typical feature of many college classes and help develop the broad skills of critical thinking, argumentation, and writing that are at the core of higher education. Both students and instructors may find themselves on solid ground with these assignments; students who are anxious about grades may also find comfort in familiar assignments and grading rubrics.

The particular format you use will of course depend on your disciplinary and pedagogical preferences and experience; we have included sample assignment guidelines with a few options later in this chapter. However you structure the assignment, most reports typically include:

- *Bill overview and background.* What problem does this bill try to solve? How does it solve it? Students should summarize the bill text and, if the legislation is long, perhaps offer a section-by-section accounting of what is contained within it. However, students should also try to grasp the larger context of the policy problem, including its history and background as well as data about its scope. Since policy problems can be framed in various ways, students should take care to present the problem in a way that suggests the bill's solution is the appropriate one to address it.
- *Advocacy position.* Why should legislators vote for this bill? Students may focus on one main argument, often related to how the policy problem is framed in the overview section, or multiple arguments. Existing advocacy efforts, the bill's sponsor, news reports, and the students' own experiences and familiarity with the problem can provide sources for these arguments. Students might also look to other states with similar bills to argue for salutary effects; the National Conference of State Legislatures and other national organizations can be helpful resources for such legislation.
- *Arguments against the bill.* Effective advocates can inform legislators of the general landscape of the law by not only advocating for a bill, but also identifying the important arguments and interests who might be aligned against it. Students should of course focus on articulating why their bill should be enacted, but they will have more effective meetings with legislators if they are familiar with the opposition,

without caricature, and have identified responses to defuse opposing arguments.

- *Stakeholders and political context.* In a similar vein to the arguments, students should identify the important stakeholders affected by their chosen legislation. What interests are activated on either side of this bill? Who is the target population, and how will they be affected? Many bills have both winners and losers, and students (and legislators) will want to be aware of both. Note that this kind of analysis may be even broken out into a separate assignment; a sample worksheet is included later in this chapter.

Depending on the comfort level and expertise of the instructor, students can also be asked to provide background and analysis on other aspects of the legislation. For example, a report might include a review of the bill's *constitutionality*. This kind of analysis can help familiarize students with the state's constitutional tradition, which is often overlooked by both citizens and scholars, and may be of particular interest to students on a prelaw track.

If possible, students should also pay attention to the bill's *fiscal impact*. Legislators almost always want to know what a bill might cost. Students and instructors may lack technical knowledge of their state's budget processes but should at least be aware of the rough costs and budgetary impact of their chosen legislation. The bill's sponsor might be able to provide some information about this; some states even require a budget analysis or impact statement with certain kinds of bills. Finally, any local experts or advisors for the class can help with resources on budget impacts—or really any aspect of the report.

There are two other considerations that may be helpful. First, you should consider the possible use of a public-facing aspect to the legislative research report . A research report can double as a policy "white paper" used in recommending a particular decision or course of action in response to a public problem. A written report that summarizes most of the information and arguments deployed by students in legislative visits can be offered to interested legislators and staffers during meetings. In most cases, this would be too much information for busy legislators, but some may share the students' passion for the bill area and a full report may "seal the deal" in winning a supportive vote.

One alternative is to put together an executive summary that provides a brief overview of the entire report, including a "recommendations" section that summarizes arguments for the bill and why to vote for it. Alternatively, you could create either a separate or alternative assignment that focuses much more on public engagement than depth of research. A "policy brief," designed much more for public consumption, can be a helpful assignment (see chapter 5, particularly the sample assignment guidelines).

And finally, as noted above, a presentation of the report's contents, either during the draft stage or after completion, should help students articulate their expertise and feel comfortable talking about their bill. The depth of research required by a typical legislative research report and presentation is almost certainly much more than they will need to draw upon for most meetings with legislators and staffers. Still, a "public" presentation of their knowledge helps scaffold those meetings and reinforce students' confidence in their own expertise. You might even invite partners and advisors to such a presentation in order to provide feedback as preparation for later legislative visits.

> *I worked at an overnight summer camp this summer and was able to explain the policy decisions surrounding state public health requirements (both Covid and non-Covid related) to campers and staff because of my knowledge of the legislative process.*
>
> —from a survey of Brandeis alumni who participated in ENACT course

One-Pager

The "one-pager" is almost universally acknowledged by professional advocates as a key component of legislative advocacy. As preparation for their visits with legislators, students should distill their research into a one- or two-page flyer. This flyer should outline their key arguments and data points; should be prepared, reviewed, and printed ahead of time; and should be attractively formatted. (While not all students are graphic designers, there are helpful models and templates as well as basic software for their use.)

There are a variety of different labels given to the advocacy flyer, including a "one-pager," "factsheet," "leave-behind," "storybook," or "storycard." Each label illuminates a part of the various purposes it serves.

- *One-Pager.* Legislators are busy, particularly in states where they serve part time or lack significant funding for staff. Advocates should be wary of overwhelming them with information; detailed research papers like the legislative research report are only helpful if requested by an office. A single sheet of paper (ideally one-sided) is widely seen as the best way to provide key advocacy points to these offices.
- *Factsheet.* No matter how ideologically polarized a state legislative environment is, evidence still matters for making the case for policy solutions. Data can be used to establish the scope of a problem and address the need for urgent action, as well as support the particular solution presented by the chosen bill.
- *Leave-Behind.* While students should create an electronic document that they can email or otherwise transfer online, they should still print paper versions of the document to literally "leave behind" them in their meetings. Providing a tangible artifact to the legislator's office has multiple benefits. Legislators often log interest in a bill, whether formally through databases or through more informal methods, and a paper flyer often ends up in a physical folder for the bill. If students meet with a legislator's staff, the flyer can be a useful artifact to help the staffer inform the legislator who will eventually make a decision on the bill.
- *Storybook/Storycard.* The storycard puts a human face on a bill or issue. It allows an advocate to tell the story of how a policy might help or hurt citizens. From an advocacy standpoint, it can be an important way to humanize the issue and to help politicians see the different kinds of people who might be impacted by a policy. Effective flyers often briefly present the story of someone who has been affected by the policy problem or solution. Working with an advocacy coalition or group can help provide such stories, as can local news stories about the problem. Stories can also come from students' personal experience.

Whether they are telling their own story or someone else's, you should consider appropriate safeguards for avoiding exploitation or exposure. Time-consuming effort is needed to find people impacted by a bill, get to know them, gain their trust, interview them, and then create the card. Having people trust students with their stories may not be possible within the time constraints of one semester. We recommend faculty use caution in sending students out to interview members of the public, as we would not want to erode trust in advocacy work in general.

One other option is to use your institution as a living laboratory. Are there campus members who have expertise in the topic or whose lived experience can enrich your students' understanding of the issue? Encourage students to seek out faculty, administrators, or other students on your campus for whom this policy might be relevant. Advise students to use campus outreach like online announcement boards, or weekly emails to find potential stakeholders. Reaching out to faculty who work in fields associated with a policy, whether healthcare, tax policy, or housing, could provide the insight and nuance needed to make storycards come alive.

When teaching the class outside of a regular session or when time does not allow making close connections with members of the public or the campus community, students may instead create a fictionalized person who represents the issue for an in-class assignment that will not be shared with the public. Of course, you should clearly communicate to all students participating in this assignment that if they are sharing any material with the public or a politician, it cannot be fictionalized, as it would be unethical. That said, students can build on their research on the issue and combine it with material gleaned from newspaper coverage and public testimony on the issue to create a composite person impacted by the policy.

Alternatively, you can separate different parts of this assignment. For example, you might ask students to develop different assignments for different purposes, distinguishing between a "policy summary" that briefly summarizes policy arguments and evidence and a separate storybook or storycard that focuses more on a personal story. This can be especially helpful if time is limited or there may be difficulty identifying and incorporating personal stories into your work for practical reasons.

Some templates are included as part of assignment guidelines later in this chapter. However, due to the variety of design, purpose, and function of these one-pager flyers, we have also included some sample one-pagers and a sample grading rubric. Again, your particular focus may reflect local advice of what appeals to legislators as well as pedagogical and curricular needs.

Additional Resources

Both you and your students can access additional resources to help with legislative research, including the following:

Legislative Database

Almost every state legislature offers an online public database for legislation. The database typically tracks key information about the bill, including sponsors, committee assignments, and status, as well as the bill text. You should familiarize yourself with your state's tracking system before introducing it to students.

Legislative Library

Many state legislatures, such as Minnesota's and Rhode Island's, feature a legislative library. These are essentially law libraries for legislators and the public and can provide resources for information about specific bills as well as the general history and operation of the legislature. Legislative librarians can be helpful resources and advisors for your ENACT class, particularly for legislative research.

Advocacy Organizations

Existing coalitions and organizations working on the chosen bill's policy issue often serve as terrific sources of information about a bill, as well as offering connections to affected communities and storytelling narratives. Still, instructors and students should be mindful of imposing burdens on such coalitions and should tread lightly.

Committee and Commission Meetings and Hearings

Some bills are introduced *sui generis* in a legislative session, but others have a long history. Some of the same legislative actors and structures, including legislators, staff, and committees, can be sources of information about a bill as well as targets for advocacy. Depending on timing, students can speak to these actors—including, as noted above, the bill's chief patron or sponsor—to gather information about the bill and policy issue before engaging in any advocacy efforts.

Research Resources

Finally, you should be reminded that legislative research is . . . research! Most academic instructors have likely developed skills and expertise in teaching research skills to students and identifying preferred resources for research projects. You should not be afraid to deploy these resources and impart these skills to students. Again, in many ways, the legislative research aspect of ENACT is one of the more familiar tools of college teaching; as a result, you might find this the easiest component of ENACT to implement.

Conclusion

ENACT classes offer students an exciting chance to engage in experiential learning, but the basic principles of higher education remain a core part of that experience. In almost all college classes, instructors guide students through bodies of knowledge in order to develop expertise in a content area, while also teaching them the skills they need to develop further expertise. ENACT is no different, and the research skills students develop in these classes build on similar efforts in other classes while also affording them the immediacy of deploying that research in real time.

Sample Assignment Guidelines for Legislative Report

Assignment. In your project teams, produce a report that identifies the problem that your bill addresses, explains how the bill proposes to solve it, evaluates the arguments for and against the bill, and recommends that legislators support the bill.

Format. Your report should include the following sections (labeled when appropriate):

[*Authors' Note: Instructors may organize this assignment in varied ways; many of the sections listed below are optional depending on the role this assignment plays in your ENACT class. Reports run from research reviews of eight to ten pages to more comprehensive overviews of the entire advocacy process (twenty to twenty-five pages). Sections, organized by different parts of the report, may include any and all of the following.*]

Report Mechanics

- *Title Page*: Include a descriptive title, authors, and affiliation.
- *Executive Summary*: Provide a brief, one-page summary of the *entire* report. This is *not* an introduction. (I encourage you to write this part after the rest of the report is fully drafted.)
- *References*: Feel free to include a separate section or use footnotes throughout the report.

Bill Overview and Background

- *Bill Overview*: Provide a section-by-section summary of the bill. Explain how the bill would change existing law and any fiscal impact on state and local governments. Describe any companion bills or similar bills also under consideration.
- *Sponsor Overview*: Identify the primary author/sponsor of the bill. Describe their district in terms of population and politics. What kinds of bills have they authored in the past? What committees do they sit on? What are their voting history and legislator ratings like?
- *Problem/Solution*: Identify the problem the bill seeks to address. (Feel free to begin with a story/anecdote that will be useful later for your storybook.) Then provide a brief overview of the specific solution laid out in the proposed bill; this may involve changes to current law or development of new laws.

Political Context and Environment

- *Comparative Context*: Have similar bills been introduced and/or passed in other states? How do other nearby states legislate on this issue?
- *Environment/Stakeholders*: Has the solution proposed by the bill been proposed in the past? If so, what happened? Identify any major stakeholders

who are in support of or in opposition to the bill; identify who might benefit and who might be hurt by the bill's passage. What, if any, impact would the bill have on the broader political landscape in the state? In what ways does the bill impact the distribution of power between groups?

Advocacy Position

- *Arguments for Your Position*: Identify the major argument(s) for your position (either supporting or opposing the bill). Why would passing this bill be a good or bad idea?
- *Arguments Against and Counters*: Identify the major arguments against your position while attributing them to opponents. ("According to wholesalers, this bill is a bad idea because . . .") Then explain why these arguments are weak, incorrect, or not as important as the arguments on your side. ("However, the wholesalers are not seeing the big picture here . . .")
- *Conclusion/Recommendations*: Provide a brief summary of the arguments above. State again the action you think legislators should take on this bill (oppose or support).

Status

[*Authors' Note: Particularly include if the final version of the report is submitted at the end of the term.*]

- *Legislative Action*: Describe the important actions that have been taken on the bill. When was the bill introduced? To which committee(s) was it referred? When did the committee(s) hold the bill's hearing? Did the bill get voted out of committee, get a floor vote, or get included in an omnibus bill? What is the status of the bill as of the due date of this report?

Sample Stakeholder Analysis Worksheet

Assignment. Use the worksheet below to conduct an analysis of the relevant actors involved in the issue your bill is addressing.

Demonstrate that you have thought about actors and their interests. Identify the relevant actors for the issue you are dealing with. This is an essential step, because you will have to analyze their interests in order to make sensible and viable policy recommendations.

Once you have identified the relevant actors, you must analyze their interests. This is important both for the context of your brief and for the critique of policy options/policy recommendations. Without a clear identification of the actors involved in the issue and their interests, your brief will be vague and useless.

Who does this issue impact? Don't simply think of the people who might usually be engaged on this issue (for example, an environmentalist for an environmental issue). Why would this be a problem for others? Why would a lot of different kinds of people care? Why would a business owner care? A soccer mom? A typical voter? A blue-collar worker?

Consider both how this problem impacts a range of people and how a proposed solution will impact them. Think about the "hero," the "villain," and the "victim," recognizing these are broad terms that don't capture the nuances of the situation. (Many issues do not have a clearly defined hero or villain—and it could be said every villain is a hero in their own mind—but this is simply a tool to think in broad terms about who stands to gain or lose from a given policy.) Add in groups that would be allies to each of them.

Focus on these specific questions:

- What is the issue?
- Who is the hero?
- Who is the villain?
- Who is the innocent victim?

Use the accompanying grid (see table 3) to identify actors and their connection to the issue.

The Person or Group	What Do You Think They Want?	Who Are Their Allies?	What Message Might Appeal to Them?

Table 3. Template for grid to identify actors and their connection to an issue.

Sample Stakeholder Analysis

What is the issue?

Plastic bags as pollution in Connecticut.

Who is the hero?

It is hard to say. The innocent victim is most often wildlife, as many of the impacts of plastic bag pollution are not felt by individuals, even when they are serious, such as the broader implications for river and ocean health or climate change. Some of the "heroes" for this issue might be advocacy groups who care about Long Island Sound, people who care about litter in their community, and people whose jobs include managing municipal waste.

Who is the villain?

While "villain" is a very strong term, people who might want there to be no restrictions on plastic bags could be those who sell or manufacture them, or those whose businesses might be hurt if they are forced to use other, biodegradable but more expensive options (like grocery stores or restaurants).

Who is the innocent victim?

The victims of plastic pollution are all of us, but the impacts are felt differently by different groups. Some of the impacts are invisible, because they are tied to pollution that happens in the middle of the ocean, air pollution in communities, or climate change. The most direct victims are species that are harmed or killed by plastic bags. Organizations that educate the public about sea life, such as an aquarium or science museum, might be good collaborators. There may also be other organizations, national or local, that have an interest in secondary issues related to the issue of plastic pollution, such as public health in general, consumer rights, environmental justice, zero waste advocates, general environmental organizations, and species-focused groups.

Sample Assignment Guidelines/Templates for One-Pager

Assignment. Students will work in project teams to produce a brief, one- or two-page summary of their stated position on their bill. One-pagers can (and probably should) be based on the same information and research used in your legislative research report , just in a more succinct manner.

Format. How you format your one-pager is up to you. This can be an opportunity to be creative! You can use color, text, and images to create an eye-catching summary. Still, keep in mind that a little goes a long way; do not make your page overly busy, use unprofessional fonts, or use any images or graphics to which you do not own the rights for distribution.

Your one-pager should include the following elements:

- *Position Statement*: The title of the summary should clearly outline your position on your chosen bill, e.g., "Vote NO on SB12!"
- *Overview*: State, in a few sentences, what the proposed bill does and why your position on the proposed bill is the right one. This can be a short narrative or bullet points.
- *Story*: Tell a good story about the bill, such as a person or organization negatively or positively affected by the proposed solution (or its absence)

The Person or Group	What Do You Think They Want?	Who Are Their Allies?	What Message Might Appeal to Them?
Environmental organization	To protect the environment.	Other environmental groups; groups focused on other environmental issues (e.g., climate change) or specific areas (e.g., a river nearby).	Focusing on the environmental impact.
Grocery stores	To reduce costs and give their customers what they want.	Restaurant owners, other shops, food delivery companies.	Finding reasonable alternatives that do not inconvenience or cost their customers more.
Those advocating for species harmed by plastic bags	To protect those species.	Organizations dedicated to other related species; educational partners like museums or aquaria.	Sharing the impact of these species. Note: Some people are more convinced by the plight of animals because they are seen as helpless; others are less convinced by a problem that impacts animals rather than humans.
Waste managers	To have effective tools for dealing with waste.	City governments that pay for waste transport or discharge; departments of sanitation and recycling.	Reducing waste is an investment in the future.

Table 4. Sample grid showing actors and their connection to an issue.

or an example of how successful a similar solution has been in other contexts (like another state).

- *Arguments/Data*: In bullet points, list a few arguments/data points in support of your position. If you can, also briefly identify counterarguments and their flaws. Think about your most compelling data and the information that will stick with policymakers.
- *Restate Position*: Conclude your summary by clearly expressing your position at the bottom of the page.
- *References*: Empirical claims, including data and stories, should be backed up by references to your sources. These should be included as footnotes/sources somewhere on the summary.

[*Authors' Note: If you wish to incorporate the "storybook" or "storycard" aspect of the one-pager, you can add some version of these additional guidelines or incorporate them into the bullet points above.*]

Interviews with Individuals Affected by the Policy Problem: We all like a good story. There is something about real stories of real people with real problems that makes us want to help, especially when we are in a place with the expertise and the power to fix the problem. For elected and appointed policymakers, good stories about a critical mass of constituents with a fixable policy problem, the campaign storybook, is an invitation to be a hero.

Your one-pager should include such a story. This story must originate from a real person through personal interviews, testimony at hearings that you attended, or informal meetings. The final product should include a distilled version of the full interview, stating the compelling essence of the story presented in a visually pleasing manner. It will be important to ask the participant's name, contact information, their willingness to talk to policymakers, and their willingness to talk to the media. It also will be important to give yourself adequate time to identify people to include in your storybook, to obtain the story, and to present it in an effective manner.

Fictionalized Story (in-class use only): As a policy advocate or in work for a nonprofit, you would be able to develop relationships over time with people impacted by a given policy. Like any relationship that requires trust, this takes time and effort. No one wants to feel like a guinea pig. It is important only to work with consenting adults who agree that you can tell their story in this format. Unfortunately, the constraints of our semester mean we do not have time to build a trusting relationship and then interview someone to find out their story.

Instead, *we will create a fictionalized person who represents the issue.* Obviously, if you were really going to share a storycard with a politician, it would be based on someone real because it would be unethical to make up a person.

The best way to do this is to read through testimony from your bill, search in local newspapers for coverage of your bill, or see how organizations advocating for your bill describe the people impacted by it. What if your bill doesn't have any testimony? Use the internet to search for a similar bill in another state. Reporters often interview people to get their perspective, whether they think a policy will hurt or help them. You can use this kind of information to create your composite person.

NOTES

1. *Americans' Dismal Views of the Nation's Politics* (Washington, DC: Pew Research Center, 2023), 87.

2. Kathryn A. DePalo, *The Failure of Term Limits in Florida* (Gainesville, FL: University Press of Florida, 2015).

3. Daniel J. Elazar, *American Federalism: A View from the States* (New York: Thomas Y. Crowell, 1966).

4. In Washington, it's a "slang term for suspending the rules to allow a bill to be advanced from second to third reading without having the bill revert to the Rules Committee." See "Glossary of Legislative Terms," Washington State Legislature, accessed July 1, 2024, https://app.leg.wa.gov/billinfo/glossary.aspx#B.

5. In Virgina, it's "the legislative day of the session, where bills must pass out of their respective chambers to be considered by the other chamber." See Janet Robey, "What Is Crossover Day?," Concerned Women of America Legislative Action Committee, last modified January 30, 2021, https://concernedwomen.org/what-is-crossover-day.

6. *Gold Standard PBL: Essential Project Design Elements* (Novato, CA: Buck Institute for Education, 2015).

Component	Superlative	Adequate	Inadequate
Problem	Substantive facts about the problem are shared in a way that is compelling and clear.	Facts about the problem are shared, but they are not very compelling or clear.	Few or no facts about the problem are shared.
Evidence	The author uses evidence to help the reader understand why they should care about the problem.	The author does not provide much evidence or does not help the reader understand why they should care about the problem.	The author neither provides evidence nor helps the reader understand why they should care about the problem.
Solutions	The author describes policy that addresses the problem. They are specific about whether the legislation will address the problem or whether changes are needed.	The author mentions policy solutions to the problem, but does not mention whether the legislation will address the problem.	The author does not mention policy solutions to the problem.
Ask	The author mentions the legislation by name and how they want the politician to vote on it.	The author either does not mention the legislation by name or does not share how they want the leader to vote on it.	The author neither mentions the legislation nor shares how they want the leader to vote on it.
Sources	Any facts shared that are not common knowledge are included as references. The citation list is consistent and of a defined style.	References to some but not all facts are noted. The citation list is consistent.	References for facts are sparse or from inappropriate sources. The citation list is inconsistent or nonexistent.
General writing and style	The author writes clearly without jargon. There are few or no errors of style or grammar. Headings, spacing, and bullet points are used to draw the eye. The piece is engaging but not too busy.	The author does not consistently express ideas clearly, using jargon or casual or unprofessional language. Font, spacing, headings, or other tools are not used consistently to increase readability.	The author does not express ideas clearly and uses inappropriate language. Few or no efforts have been made to make the piece reader-friendly.
Contact	The author shares contact information.	The author shares contact information.	The author does not share contact information.

Table 5. Sample One-Pager Grading Rubric.

FIGURE 3.2. One-Pager Template 1: Policy Focus.

[USE THE PERSON'S NAME] STORY

The Issue

In just a few lines share why this issue is important.

Xs Story

- Help the reader understand how this person is impacted by the issue.
- Anecdotal evidence or the person's perspective over time can enrich the story you are trying to tell.
- Use data to tie this person's story to the larger picture-- who do they represent.

The Solution

- What is the policy of interest?
- How does the policy address the problem?
- If improvements to the policy are recommended, include that here.

Photo credit here: By Paul Einerhand, Free to use through Unsplash license

CALL TO ACTION!

What should the politician do?

SOURCES

Share your sources.
Only use photographs with permission, or for fictionalized accounts, those with an open license.
Try resources like unsplash.com and select "free" images.

CONTACT INFORMATION

FIGURE 3.3. One-Pager Template 2: Story Focus.

SOLVING THE PLASTIC BAG PROBLEM IN CONNECTICUT

KATHARINE OWENS

Did you know?

- More than 350 million tons of plastic is produced every year [1].
- The oceans contain "a minimum of 5.25 trillion particles" of plastic [2].
- 95% of plastic packaging globally is not recycled [3], and
- 90.5 % of all plastic ever made has never been recycled [4].

Image credit: Canva

DIRTY BEACHES COST MONEY, CLEAN BEACHES MAKE MONEY!

A study of 31 California beaches found that reducing pollution by 50% at beaches in Orange County could generate $67 million in benefits to Orange County residents over a 3-month period[5].

Image credit: Canva

WHAT CAN WE DO?

- Bag banning policies work.
- Plastic bag policies can take the form of reductions, limitations on use, outright bans, and taxes on bags [6].
- HB1: An Act to Ban Plastic Bags is a comprehensive policy that will effectively eliminate plastic bags in Connecticut by 2027.

Image credit: Canva

YOUR SUPPORT MATTERS!

We can protect Connecticut's industry, people, and wildlife in the Long Island Sound by banning bags.

Please support House Bill 1: An Act to Ban Plastic Bags.

SOURCES

[1] PLASTICSEUROPE (2022) PLASTICS: THE FACTS. AVAILABLE ONLINE: HTTPS://PLASTICSEUROPE.ORG/KNOWLEDGE-HUB/PLASTICS-THE-FACTS-2022/
[2] ERIKSEN, M., ET AL. (2014) PLASTIC POLLUTION IN THE WORLD'S OCEANS: MORE THAN 5 TRILLION PLASTIC PIECES WEIGHING OVER 250,000 TONS AFLOAT AT SEA. PLOS ONE 9, 12: E111913.
[3] AGENDA, I. (2016, JANUARY). THE NEW PLASTICS ECONOMY RETHINKING THE FUTURE OF PLASTICS. IN THE WORLD ECONOMIC FORUM: GENEVA, SWITZERLAND (VOL. 36).
[4] GEYER, R., JAMBECK, J. R., & LAW, K. L. (2017). PRODUCTION, USE, AND FATE OF ALL PLASTICS EVER MADE. SCIENCE ADVANCES, 3(7), E1700782.
[5] LEGGETT, C., SCHERER, N., CURRY, M., BAILEY, R., & HAAS, T. (2014). ASSESSING THE ECONOMIC BENEFITS OF REDUCTIONS IN MARINE DEBRIS: A PILOT STUDY OF BEACH RECREATION IN ORANGE COUNTY, CALIFORNIA. NOAA MAR DEBRIS PROGR IND ECON INC, 45.
[6] DUKE UNIVERSITY'S NICHOLAS INSTITUTE FOR ENERGY, ENVIRONMENT, AND SUSTAINABILITY MAINTAINS AN ONLINE PLASTICS POLICY INVENTORY WITH EXAMPLE POLICIES FROM AROUND THE COUNTRY AND THE WORLD: NICHOLAS INSTITUTE FOR ENERGY, ENVIRONMENT, AND SUSTAINABILITY (2024). PLASTICS POLICY INVENTORY. AVAILABLE ONLINE: HTTPS://NICHOLASINSTITUTE.DUKE.EDU/PLASTICS-POLICY-INVENTORY

Please contact me with any questions: Katharine Owens
myemail@emailaddress (860) 555-1234

Examples of effective one-page summaries of a stated position on proposed legislation. *Continued→*

GILS'S STORY

The Issue

Plastic pollution in public waterways is a global problem.

- More than 350 million tons of plastic is produced every year [1].
- The oceans contain "a minimum of 5.25 trillion particles" of plastic [2].

Gil's Story

Gil Gillman of Norwich, Connecticut has worked in fisheries his whole life. His family-owned company, Gillman Fisheries, has been operating in the state since 1938. Gil reports that he has noticed a sharp increase of plastic pollution over his lifetime, especially bags, which foul the nets and motors of boats working in the Long Island Sound. Gil supports House Bill 1 because it will improve conditions for his company and for hundreds of other fishery-related industries in Connecticut. The fisheries sector in Connecticut is a 15 million dollar per year industry [3].

The Solution

Bag banning policies have led to decreases in bag pollution around the world [4].

HB1: An Act to Ban Plastic Bags is a comprehensive policy that will effectively eliminate plastic bags in Connecticut by 2027.

Photo by Paul Einerhand. Free to use through Unsplash license

CALL TO ACTION!

Support fishermen like Gil Gillman by voting in favor of **House Bill 1: An Act to Ban Plastic Bags.**

SOURCES

[1] PlasticsEurope (2022) Plastics: The Facts. Available online: https://plasticseurope.org/knowledge-hub/plastics-the-facts-2022/

[2] Eriksen, M., et al. (2014) Plastic pollution in the world's oceans: more than 5 trillion plastic pieces weighing over 250,000 tons afloat at sea. PloS One 9, 12: e111913.

[3] https://seagrant.uconn.edu/focus-areas/sustainable-fisheries/#:~:text=Connecticut's%20commercial%20fishing%20sector%20is,vessel%20value%20of%20%2415.4%20million.

[4] Maes, Thomas, J. Barry, H. A. Leslie, A. D. Vethaak, E. E. M. Nicolaus, R. J. Law, B. P. Lyons, R. Martinez, B. Harley, and J. E. Thain. (2018). Below the surface: Twenty-five years of seafloor litter monitoring in coastal seas of North West Europe (1992–2017). Science of the total environment 630: 790-798

Photo source: Paul Einerhand on Unsplash https://unsplash.com/s/photos/fishery?license=free

Please contact me with any questions: Katharine Owens
myemail@emailaddress (860) 555-1234

Assignment B: Storybook

THE PROBLEM

BACKGROUND

Drought in Massachusetts is an ongoing problem. In 2022, the entire Commonwealth was in a severe drought. This will get worse with climate change, as periods of drought extend. All municipalities draw water from the same aquifer. If this is depleted, the Commonwealth will run out of water.

SIGNIFICANCE

- We all need to water to live; drought keeps us from having enough.
- Drought response has not been equal. Some municipalities are forced to conserve while others are not.
- Our progeny deserve adequate access to water.

MA DROUGHT IN 2022

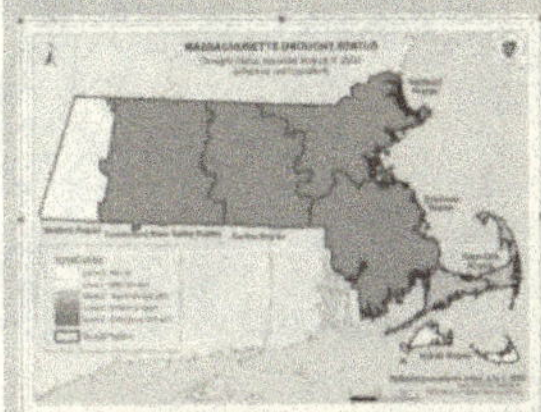

SPONSORS

Representative Joan Meschino
3rd Plymouth District
Joan.Meschino@mahouse.gov

Senator James B. Eldridge
Middlesex and Worcester
James@Jameseldridge.com

H. 861/S. 475

AN ACT RELATIVE TO MAINTAINING ADEQUATE WATER SUPPLIES THROUGH EFFECTIVE DROUGHT MANAGEMENT

HEAR THEIR STORIES

COLLEEN HITCHCOCK

ASSOCIATE PROFESSOR OF BIOLOGY AND ENVIRONMENTAL STUDIES PROGRAM CHAIR, BRANDEIS UNIVERSITY

Professor Colleen Hitchcock argues that if we reduce our watering of lawns, in addition to other measures, we can vastly increase the Commonwealth's climate resilience.

"ANYBODY WHO IS WATERING THEIR LAWN IS OVERUSING WATER."

ZEUS SMITH

POLICY ADVOCATE, CHARLES RIVER WATERSHED ASSOCIATION

Zeus Smith describes this bill as one of plain common sense. He explains that the measures proposed in the bill can improve inequality in the Commonwealth. He adds that this bill will prevent the Commonwealth from running out of water in both the long- and short-term.

"THERE IS A PROFOUND SENSE AMONG CITIZENS . . . OF A LACK OF EQUITY WHEN YOU GO INTO A TOWN THAT HAS SPRINKLERS RUNNING BECAUSE THEY'RE ON A PRIVATE WELL, AND YOU'RE ON A PRETTY STRICT DROUGHT CONSERVATION MEASURE."

HOW DOES THE BILL ADDRESS DROUGHT?

SUMMARY OF BILL

- Gives power to the Governor to appoint a drought management task force
- Applies drought provisions equally across the Commonwealth, ensuring equity across municipalities

WHY SHOULD I VOTE FOR IT?

- Protect our most precious resource, water
- Resolve inequality across municipalities
- Ensure future generations have an adequate water supply

Massachusetts Rivers Alliance

Charles River Watershed Association

Continued→

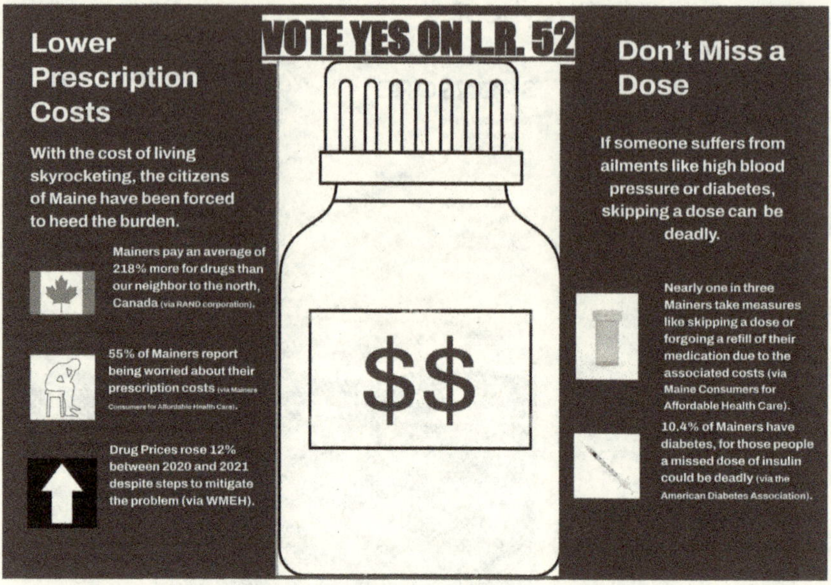
Lower Prescription Costs
With the cost of living skyrocketing, the citizens of Maine have been forced to heed the burden.
Mainers pay an average of 218% more for drugs than our neighbor to the north, Canada (via RAND corporation).
55% of Mainers report being worried about their prescription costs (via Mainers Consumers for Affordable Health Care).
Drug Prices rose 12% between 2020 and 2021 despite steps to mitigate the problem (via WMEH).
VOTE YES ON L.R. 52
$$
Don't Miss a Dose
If someone suffers from ailments like high blood pressure or diabetes, skipping a dose can be deadly.
Nearly one in three Mainers take measures like skipping a dose or forgoing a refill of their medication due to the associated costs (via Maine Consumers for Affordable Health Care).
10.4% of Mainers have diabetes, for those people a missed dose of insulin could be deadly (via the American Diabetes Association).

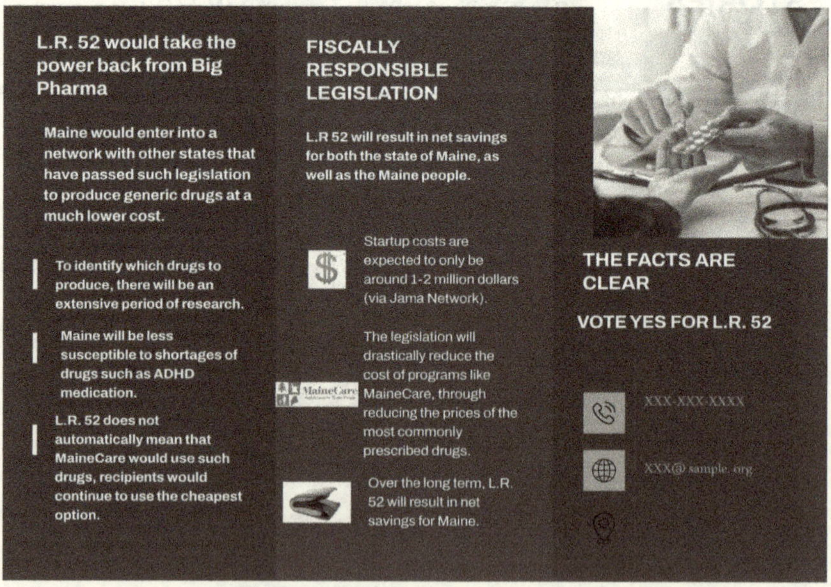
L.R. 52 would take the power back from Big Pharma
Maine would enter into a network with other states that have passed such legislation to produce generic drugs at a much lower cost.
To identify which drugs to produce, there will be an extensive period of research.
Maine will be less susceptible to shortages of drugs such as ADHD medication.
L.R. 52 does not automatically mean that MaineCare would use such drugs, recipients would continue to use the cheapest option.
FISCALLY RESPONSIBLE LEGISLATION
L.R 52 will result in net savings for both the state of Maine, as well as the Maine people.
Startup costs are expected to only be around 1-2 million dollars (via Jama Network).
The legislation will drastically reduce the cost of programs like MaineCare, through reducing the prices of the most commonly prescribed drugs.
Over the long term, L.R. 52 will result in net savings for Maine.
THE FACTS ARE CLEAR
VOTE YES FOR L.R. 52
XXX-XXX-XXXX
XXX@ sample. org

Save Lives with HB 637

Protect Virginia's First Responders & Roadside Workers

OVERVIEW OF HB 637:

HB 637 establishes the following:

- Minimum $500 fine for drivers who fail to abide by "Move Over" law.
- Requires operators who cannot change lanes to pass at a speed no greater than 10 miles per hour.

LT. BRAD CLARK

Lt. Clark was a firefighter with Hanover County Fire & EMS that was struck on the side of I-295 on the night of October 11th, 2018, leaving behind a wife, children, and countless colleagues. The driver of the tractor trailer failed to move over for stopped emergency vehicles, a choice that ultimately ended Lt. Clark's life.

KEY FACTS

- On Average, **24 Emergency Responders are killed** each year while working on roadside scenes. [Auto Club]
- From **2003 - 2019, 2,103 Construction Workers lost their lives** on the side of the road. [CDC]

Protect Virginians on the Roadside!
Vote "Yes" on HB 637

Spencer Willett - SpencerWillett@go.rmc.edu
Alex Fearnow - AlexFearnow@go.rmc.edu
Christopher Kendall - ChristopherKendall@go.rmc.edu

Find Out More: https://linktr.ee/HB637

4 Meeting with Legislators

For most students, the visits to the capitol are the most exciting, though anxiety-producing, components of the ENACT course.

It makes sense that these visits would bring up big feelings for our students. Capitol buildings are meant to be grand. Their architecture and décor are meant to communicate authority, importance, and wealth. The people who work in the legislature, whether they are legislators, staff, or lobbyists, signal their importance and status in numerous ways, from their use of formal titles and insider acronyms to their professional attire and the fast pace at which they do their work. Interacting with important people in important buildings on important issues is what draws students to the ENACT course. It's also what can make this course feel so risky for students.

Likewise, for an instructor, ENACT courses entail unique challenges and opportunities. In a traditional, classroom-based course, you have greater control over the environment in which your students learn. You select the course materials and assessments. You design activities that mostly take place within the contained environment of the classroom. You can expect a certain amount of ease with your students, as they are likely familiar with the expectations of the classroom environment. In ENACT courses, you don't have as much control over the learning conditions of your students. You may assign a common course textbook, but much of what students are reading will be specific to their issues and bills. You'll design activities and assessments, but these will likely rely at least partially on legislators, legislative staff, and others at the capitol, which means things may not go as planned. The capitol environment will be foreign to most, if not all, of your students—and maybe even to you—which means you'll need to invest a significant amount of time in explicit instruction in institutional norms, as well as in preparing students for the emotional highs and lows of working in the capitol environment. For both students and instructors, the ENACT course requires us to learn new skills and take new risks, while opening us up to the possibility of new rewards: new feelings of empowerment, meaning, and significance unique to participating in (not just thinking about) politics.

In this chapter, we'll discuss how to prepare students for their work with legislators at the capitol to ensure their experiences are as empowering as possible. We will present activities you can include in your course to build community among students, to build confidence at the capitol, and to help students think about what it means to represent communities at the legislature. We will also provide an overview of the meeting script and elevator speech assignments.

Key Questions

What are the demographic characteristics of your legislators and legislative staff?

When planning your ENACT course, one of the first things you will want to find out about your capitol is who is working there. Specifically, who are the legislators and legislative staff? What demographic groups do they come from? To what extent do the demographic characteristics of the people working in the capitol—including lobbyists and other non-state employees—reflect the demographic characteristics of your state and your students? It is important for you as the instructor to have a sense of who your students will see represented at the capitol, so that you are prepared to help them make sense of not only who is present at or absent from the capitol, but also *why* some groups are overrepresented, while others are underrepresented or not represented at all.

Unfortunately, gathering demographic information about your state legislature may be difficult. Your state legislature may not publish data on the demographic characteristics of legislators and staff. For lobbyists and other non-state employees who regularly do their work at the capitol, it's unlikely that you will be able to access any demographic information. However, you may be able to find some information in the local news media. Alternatively, you may be able to get information on the demographic characteristics of legislators with the assistance of your legislator or their legislative assistant. Some state legislatures have caucuses based on identities; for example, the

Minnesota State Legislature includes a People of Color and Indigenous Caucus and a Queer Caucus.[1] Members of identity-based caucuses and their legislative assistants may be able to help you informally gather data on the demographic characteristics of the state legislators.

Once you have a sense of which demographic groups are represented in the legislature, you'll also want to include readings in your course materials that help students understand not only *who* makes up the legislators, but *why*. It's important for students to understand the ways in which campaign finance laws, electoral institutions, and informal professional networks give some groups (for example, white, wealthy, professional-class people) advantages in running for office, while making it more difficult for members of other groups to run for office, win, and serve.

It is particularly important to attend to the role of economic class at the legislature, both in terms of the structural barriers for working-class and people of lower incomes in running for office and in terms of the dominant class culture at the capitol. While it has become increasingly common for universities to require students to learn about racial and ethnic diversity, and perhaps even gender and sexual diversity, students are far less likely to have had the opportunity to learn about class cultures in the United States. Helping students understand class cultures and their divergent norms of behavior and language will be important for preparing them to do their work at the capitol. Resources for helping students understand institutional and cultural barriers to equal representation at the capitol are included in the Resources section below.

What are the demographic characteristics of your students?

It is difficult to overstate how important feelings of *belonging* are for student success. When students feel they belong in our institutions, they show up differently. They are more engaged in course work and discussions. They are more likely to persist to graduation. In ENACT courses, instructors must work to cultivate students' feelings of belonging not only on their college campuses but also at the capitol. This work requires us to know who our students are: what communities they are a part of, what identities are important to them. Knowing who our students are is an important prerequisite for explicitly cultivating feelings of belonging for all our students at the capitol, especially those who are more likely to be underrepresented or unrepresented at the capitol.

One of the most powerful signals students will receive about whether they belong at the capitol is whether they see people like them there. Some students are more likely than others to recognize people like them at the capitol, particularly white, upper-middle-class men. Others, like women, people of color, and students with invisible but marginalized identities, may have more difficulty in finding people they identify with on the capitol campus. As instructors, we can help our students cultivate feelings of belonging by proactively connecting our students with legislators and legislative staff from their communities, with their shared identities.

Race, gender, sexuality, citizenship status, and class are likely to be especially salient identities for students at the capitol. You can help students cultivate feelings of belonging at the capitol by inviting legislators who share communities and identities with your students to speak to the class *before* students begin their advocacy work. It is important to note that even if your students are likely to see themselves represented at the capitol, you should still invite legislators from underrepresented communities to speak with the class. Aside from cultivating belonging, meeting with legislators of diverse backgrounds provides all students the opportunity to consider which groups are overrepresented, underrepresented, or not represented at all in their state legislatures. Descriptive representation is an important concept for students of all backgrounds when considering the quality of democratic decision-making in their state. The panel discussion with legislators activity described below is one model for formally including legislators in class discussions about the importance of representation for all communities. This activity can be useful for both cultivating feelings of belonging for underrepresented groups and for evaluating the representativeness of your state legislature.

How many class sessions can you spend at the capitol?

As you are planning your ENACT course, you will want to consider how many class sessions you can spend at the capitol. In general, the more the better. Ideally, you will have multiple class sessions at the capitol before students begin their advocacy activities with legislators and legislative staff.

These pre-advocacy class visits allow students to become acquainted with and acclimated to the capitol. By spending time at the capitol prior to their advocacy meetings, students have the opportunity to learn the layout of the capitol so they can confidently make their way to meetings. Likewise, you give them the opportunity to see the cultural norms of the institution in action, which makes it possible for students to make strategic decisions about how they want to appear and speak in their interactions with legislators and legislative staff. Students who only visit the capitol on the day of a meeting with a legislator are less likely to feel comfortable at the capitol, and therefore more likely to feel anxious during their meeting. Some ENACT course models even include an "orientation" visit during the first week of class to try to immediately demystify the capitol and provide context for student work throughout the course.

By giving students multiple opportunities to be on the capitol campus before they begin their advocacy work, you'll set students up for more successful, productive meetings with legislators and their staff. Some examples of capitol-based activities that can increase students' comfort at the capitol are the capitol tour and panel discussion with legislators activities described below.

What if your campus is far from your state capitol?

As mentioned earlier in this volume, resource and logistical constraints may make it difficult to engage with legislators at the capitol, as very few institutions of higher education are conveniently located near the statehouse. In this regard, ENACT is probably similar to other class experiences that might require resources and travel. And as with any field trip, instructors might need to be creative to draw on campus resources in order to fund and schedule travel. If the capitol is far enough away, you may even have to consider the risks and rewards of managing overnight travel with students. If you are lucky enough to have support for advance planning, such as a trip to the capitol a semester or so before your ENACT course launch, you can more easily plan travel logistics and make the necessary contacts.

If travel constraints limit your ENACT students to one visit during the term, we encourage you to arrange significant structure for that single visit in order to have the best experience possible. You could schedule class activities like the tour or panel described in this chapter or arrange for orientation sessions with friendly legislators and staffers. For a single-day visit, you might structure activities in the morning and let students loose for legislative visits in the afternoon; a multiday visit might have more structure on the first day, with a second day allocated solely for office visits and attending committee hearings.

If scheduling an in-person visit seems difficult, you should consider options for virtual visits. During the Covid-19 pandemic, many state legislatures moved to incorporate virtual meetings of various kinds. Some legislatures and individual legislative offices may still accommodate such visits, while others allow public comments and testimony in committee hearings through virtual participation. We strongly recommend traveling to the capitol when feasible, for a variety of reasons that should be clear throughout both this chapter and the entire book. Still, virtual options may expand the possibility of participation for your students.

How should students plan their legislative visits?

There are a number of different ways that students can engage with the legislature, and you should provide structured guidance and opportunities in your classroom to consider options and plan legislative visits ahead of time. As noted throughout this volume, the logistical constraints on your time at the legislature—class timing, session length, distance, number of trips, etc.—will shape these discussions and activities.

The rules and norms of your state legislature will particularly matter in how you approach the logistics of student visits. Do legislators have daily committee or caucus meetings at certain times? Is there a set schedule or does the daily activity of your legislature vary widely? Is there a norm of making appointments or are legislative offices more free-wheeling? In some contexts, students might be best served by arriving at the legislature with a list of offices in some rough priority order, and they can just see who is available. In others, particularly if there are opportunities for multiple visits to the capitol, students should prepare a more formal schedule that includes committee hearings and opportunities for testimony.

Throughout the scheduling process, you should provide guidance and scaffolding for students. Some of this can be logistical; students from varied backgrounds and especially of traditional college age may have little experience with tasks like calling an office and making an appointment, and instructors should not assume familiarity with these norms. Sample scripts and emails and mock calls may help students gain familiarity and comfort with these logistics. More importantly, you should reinforce the students' views about their rights and privileges as constituents, residents, and advocates. Their requests for meetings are not impositions but important opportunities for both them and the legislative office to engage in a vital component of civic life. The more comfortable they become with this idea, the more prepared and empowered students are to take roles as community advocates later in their lives.

What are the norms of behavior at the capitol, and will your students be familiar with them?

Students' comfort and empowerment may become even more of a concern as you move into the physical space of the statehouse. The principles of democracy would suggest that all people should feel welcome and valued in our state capitols. Unfortunately, this is not the case. State capitols can be intimidating environments. The grandeur of the architecture along with the norms of formality at the capitol can make some students feel out of place. Students with working-class and low-income backgrounds may feel especially uncomfortable at the capitol, as norms about dress and speech tend to represent the values and perspectives of middle- and upper-middle-class people. Although one shouldn't need to own a business suit or speak white, middle-class English to feel like they belong at the capitol, the fact remains that those who do will have an easier time blending into the environment.

State capitols may vary in terms of the expected level of formality. It is up to the instructor of an ENACT course to determine how formal the environment is before bringing students to the capitol. Spending time at the capitol and observing legislative staff, committee meetings, and other capitol business can be helpful for getting a sense of the cultural expectations and norms. If you're unsure of the expectations at the capitol—for instance, regarding dress code or use of formal titles for legislators and staff—you may want to reach out to the legislative assistant for one of your legislators to find out what is expected behavior at the capitol.

Once you feel confident you understand the behavioral norms at the capitol, it is important to have explicit conversations about those norms with your students. It's particularly important to discuss how the norms of the capitol are culturally specific and represent cultural expectations associated with particular groups—typically, white, middle- and upper-middle-class professionals. The point of these conversations is not to insist that students adopt the culturally specific norms, but rather to ensure they understand what the expectations will be at the capitol so that they can make strategic decisions about how to engage with lawmakers and legislative staff. Some students may choose to dress and speak in ways that are more aligned with the norms of the capitol. Others may decide that showing up as their full selves—in clothing that feels authentic to them, speaking in ways that express their own cultural location—better expresses their values. As an instructor, you can prepare students to make independent, informed decisions about how they want to present themselves when interacting with professionals at the capitol.

> *This course taught me that I have power and it enabled me to grasp the difference any single person can make through involvement in local politics, either by running for office or being a citizen advocate. . . . Although at times the legislative process is slow and discouraging, and immediate results are hard to come by, it is important to be patient and maintain passion and persistence necessary to effect change.*
>
> Marian Gardner, Brandeis University

How can you proactively cultivate community among your students to help them support each other in taking risks?

ENACT courses require students to learn new skills and take new risks. In our courses, they learn how to navigate the legislature's information systems—whether that's learning how to track legislation on the legislature's website, learning how to conduct research in the special collections of the legislative library, or learning about the research offices at the capitol and how to make requests for information. They learn how to write new kinds of documents, from elevator speeches and meeting scripts to one-pagers and legislative briefs. While their coursework in other classes will likely have given them some transferable skills, the unique context of the ENACT course requires them to take on kinds of work with which they will likely be unfamiliar. In addition, ENACT courses ask students to develop some comfort speaking authoritatively on important public issues. While some students may feel very entitled to speak with authority, others struggle, often due to experiencing stigmatization as nondominant group members. To adequately prepare students to take the risks ENACT courses require of them, you should work to develop community with and among students.

When instructors build relationships and create community in their classes, they empower students to take risks they might otherwise be too intimidated to attempt. In ENACT courses, students work in teams on their advocacy projects, which might result in feelings of trust and concern. However, working in teams on its own isn't enough to ensure students develop the kinds of relationships that will lead to feelings of efficacy and empowerment. Therefore, it's important for you to devote time and attention to developing relationships with and among students.

To ensure students are equipped to support each other throughout the semester, ENACT instructors can practice both individual and group check-ins as part of their weekly class meetings. During individual check-ins, everyone in the class community (including the instructor) shares how they are feeling coming into class that day. Everyone also has the opportunity to share anything that's impacting their ability to be present in class that day or keep up with the coursework. You also can include group check-ins. During the group check-ins, each group has an opportunity to discuss both their obstacles and accomplishments since the last group check-in. The group check-in gives students the opportunity to voice concerns and strategize with the instructor and other students about how to complete their work. These discussions can help reduce tension in the group, normalize encountering obstacles, and generate feelings of togetherness as a team, as students come up with strategies together. Individual and group check-ins are described in more detail in the Assignments section of the chapter.

Additionally, you can normalize relationships of care and concern by regularly and repeatedly reminding students they understand the unique emotional challenges that are part of the class. Students in the ENACT course not only learn many new skills and complete many new kinds of assignments, but they also take on unique identity risks in the class. When students meet with legislators, their aides, and others at the capitol to advocate for their bills, it becomes necessary for them to speak with authority about their bill. They must become experts on their bill and be ready to explain and answer questions about it.

Inhabiting the role of an expert can feel very risky for students. They are likely to feel less confident reading and interpreting the legal language in which the bill is written. The capitol environment may make any non-dominant identities they hold particularly salient. As a result, students may feel particularly uncomfortable speaking with authority in meetings with capitol professionals. As such, it is important for you to normalize these feelings and help students develop strategies for successfully conducting their meetings, as well as coping mechanisms for when things do not go as planned. Acknowledging that speaking as an expert can feel intimidating and developing explicit plans for how students can support each other in their teams through the discomfort helps build community in the course and can help students feel empowered to take risks at the capitol.

How can you model adaptability and responsiveness for your students?

State capitols are dynamic spaces. Schedules can be unpredictable. Hearing dates get rescheduled. Priorities shift in the legislature over the course of the session. Legislators' schedules change in response to the many pressures they have on their time. As a result, instructors and students in ENACT courses must be prepared to adapt to changing circumstances at the capitol. To prepare students to be responsive to shifts at the capitol, you need to discuss the factors that make capitols such dynamic places and model adaptability and responsiveness when interacting with legislators and other capitol professionals.

For example, if you attempt to organize the panel discussion with legislators activity mentioned above, you will almost certainly have the opportunity to model adaptability for your students. To have a successful panel conversation, it is likely that you will need to invite and confirm as many as double the number of speakers you hope will attend. On the day of the event, it is very likely that even confirmed speakers will need to drop out at the last minute. Perhaps they had an unexpected meeting scheduled with a constituent. Or they may be the author of a bill and their hearing for it got moved onto the schedule for that day. There are many reasons that a legislator, even one who confirmed their participation, may not be able to attend. If you gracefully adapt and generously explain a speaker's absence, this can help normalize for students how often plans change at the capitol and model how to respond when things do not go as planned.

Likewise, the variability of the legislative calendar and legislative schedule will impact students' ability to complete certain assignments "on time." Students' ability to access some of the information required to complete the assignment will be dependent on the bill's progress at the legislature. As a result, students will likely feel the hurry-up-and-wait energy that is so typical at state capitols. They may have little they can do on their legislative research report for weeks. Then, once their bill gets a hearing, they may have an overwhelming number of documents, videos, and testimonies to sort through. Preparing students for the unpredictability of the capitol and adapting assignments and due dates to reflect that unpredictability is an important part of running a successful ENACT course.

Assignments and Other Key Course Components

Below is a discussion of several components of the ENACT course that are designed to prepare students for meetings with legislators. Each of these components is meant to increase students' feelings of community, belonging, and/or expertise at the capitol, which helps prepare them for an empowering experience.

Individual and Group Check-Ins

Individual and group check-ins are an important tool for building community in your ENACT course. By asking students how they are doing and giving them space to share what is happening in their lives—both in and out of the ENACT course—you demonstrate that you care for them as whole human beings and are invested in their well-being. Further, you give students the opportunity to learn about each other and come to care for one another. The individual check-in can be incorporated into any class as a community-building activity but is especially important in ENACT courses. The group check-ins are more specific to active learning experiences like the ENACT course.

Instructors who want to include the individual check-ins in their course can begin each class session by having students answer the following questions:

- How are you feeling coming into class today?
- Is there anything you need from us to feel fully supported in being present today?

These questions give students the opportunity to reflect on their mental/emotional state as they enter the class. This can help them feel grounded and bring all their attention to their current experience of the classroom.

In general, it's helpful for you to model how to answer these questions during the initial check-ins of the semester. By modeling for students the kinds of answers that might be shared, you help students feel less awkward about sharing and less confused about how to answer the questions. For example, you might offer these answers to the questions: "I'm feeling good coming into class today and I am excited to be with you all. I'm also a little tired because I have been working too much and haven't gotten enough rest. In order for me to feel fully supported in being present today, I'm going to need everyone to bring their best energy to our conversation. And I might need some more caffeine!"

By sharing an answer like this, students see that the question is about how we're feeling and that it is okay to share our emotions. An answer like this also acknowledges that we are all whole human beings with lives outside of the classroom that impact our ability to be present and prepared for class meetings. By modeling this for students, you help them reflect on their own mental/emotional state and how it influences their experience in the course. Further, you normalize that people have varying levels of capacity day-to-day and emphasize that we can depend on the others in the classroom community to support us when we're not at our best. This is an especially important reminder for a course that depends so much on teamwork.

Group check-ins are an opportunity for teams to reflect on their progress completing the many tasks and assignments associated with the advocacy project. They are also an opportunity to address any obstacles or issues that are coming up for the group. It's common for students to run into roadblocks as they are attempting to book advocacy meetings with legislators or gather information about their bill, its author, and their district. They may encounter an unresponsive legislative assistant. Or they may need support in identifying who at the capitol can answer their questions about their bill. These group check-ins are an opportunity for students to voice these concerns, especially so they do not get stuck, letting anxiety build and time slip by. In the group check-ins, students answer the following questions each week:

- What have you been able to get done over the last week?
- What obstacles are you encountering that are preventing you from making more progress on the assignments? How can I help you get what you need to keep going?
- How are each of you feeling about your ability to contribute to the group right now?

The last question is important because it gives students the opportunity to reflect on their current capacity in conversation with their teammates. Sometimes with group work, students can struggle to stay in communication with their teammates. When this happens, resentment can build among them. Giving each team member the opportunity to reflect on how they are showing up for their teammates and share any personal obligations or struggles that are getting in the way of their best work can help defuse the situation. It also provides an opportunity to work with the team to strategize how they can distribute and redistribute the workload among them over the course of the semester as unforeseen obstacles arise. It is important that we ask students to assess their own contributions to the team, rather than others' contributions. By asking students to be critically reflective about themselves, we lessen the likelihood that they will explain group challenges in terms of others' failures and instead consider their own role in creating the group dynamic.

Capitol Tour

Capitol buildings are cultural artifacts that can be interpreted in multiple ways. Your state capitol very likely offers a tour. Typically, the tours offered by capitol staff tend to focus on the history of the capitol building itself—when it was built, the provenance of the capitol art and décor, any significant changes to the building over time. However, you can consider providing your own, alternative tour of the capitol. On this tour, the goal is to read the building narratively, rather than historically. The main question you'll work to answer with your students is, "Whose story is being told in the design of this building and whose stories are absent?" This activity offers significant context for ENACT work, with the primary benefit of getting students to think critically about the significance of demographic groups and descriptive representation at the capitol over time. It also has a secondary benefit of giving students the opportunity to become acquainted with the layout and feel of the capitol campus before having to navigate it on their own for their meetings.

Preparing for the capitol tour will require a significant amount of time and effort ahead of the class. You will have to learn about the building itself, as well as the art and décor within the building. You may need to spend a lot of time in the building, becoming familiar with the paintings, reflecting on their subject matter, noticing who is represented and who is absent in them, noticing who are the protagonists and who are background characters (or worse). You may need to learn the artists who produced the work, as well as the works' titles. You should also apply these steps to any statuary on the capitol grounds.

As you prepare for the narrative capitol tour activity, you may want to ask yourself the following questions:

- What style of architecture is the building? What kinds of values, perspectives, or ideas are expressed in the building's design?
- How formal is the décor of the building? What is meant to be communicated to the viewer through the decoration of the building?
- What types of art are present at the capitol? Can the artworks be broken into types or collections? If so, how could each type be described?
- Who is represented in the artwork and how are they represented? If there is more than one person in the artwork, who is the main character and who is relegated to the background? What is the power relationship between the people or groups represented in the image?
- What do the titles of the artworks tell us about the social location or perspective of the artist? The assumed viewer? What themes emerge when we consider the titles of the artworks together?

- How is symbolism employed in the artworks and what do the symbolic meanings of the works tell us about the values, perspectives, or ideas represented in the work?
- Which cultural histories or perspectives are represented in the artworks? Are there groups in our state who would not find their histories or perspectives represented in the artworks? Or, worse, are there groups in our state who would find their representation in the artworks offensive or misrepresentative of their group?
- How do these artworks collectively tell the story of our state? Which people and groups are treated as the active agents in making the history of our state? Whose contributions are unrepresented or even misrepresented?
- What do the answers to the questions above tell us about who is meant to feel welcome in the capitol buildings? Who does the artwork assume will be viewing these images as they do their work in the capitol?
- Who do you actually see at the capitol? What are the observable demographic characteristics of the legislators, their staff, and others working there? If you attend a hearing, which demographic groups are represented in the meeting—as audience, as testifiers, and as committee members? Who do you notice is absent from the capitol or underrepresented?

At the end of the tour, students have an opportunity to discuss their answers to the questions listed above. They discuss who the presumed audience is for these images and what that says about who is expected to be present at the capitol and making decisions for our state. They discuss the demographic characteristics of the people they've seen at the capitol that day and reflect on why some groups are present and others are absent. At the end of the tour, each student answers the following question: "Now that we've spent some time attending to the story that our capitol tells us, what does it feel like or mean for you to be here?" By answering this question, students have the opportunity to reflect on the significance of their presence at the capitol. This can be an especially powerful reflection opportunity for students, particularly for those who come from communities that are more likely to be underrepresented or absent from the capitol grounds on any given day. A sample tour for a particular state is included later in this chapter as a model.

> *As an African American woman, there is a certain level of distrust that comes in when thinking about the government and what they are doing to help my community. With the class I got to talk to a lot of people in legislation that had similar ideals and standards as me. So those were reassuring to me.*
>
> —response from ENACT survey, Brandeis University

Panel Discussion with Legislators Activity

The panel discussion with legislators is an excellent activity to follow the capitol tour activity. Both activities are focused on the concept of representation. In the capitol tour activity, the focus is primarily on figurative representation in the artworks. In the panel discussion with legislators activity, representation takes on another meaning. Here, we're primarily concerned with how legislators understand what it means to represent their communities, whether that is constituents in their districts or other demographic groups they represent. By bringing select legislators together to speak with students in a panel format, you and your students can directly address these questions with legislators while giving students a chance to interact with them in a less intimidating environment than an advocacy meeting.

To run the panel discussion with legislators activity, you ideally will be able to reserve a room on the capitol campus. Having a room reserved at the capitol makes it easier for legislators to attend. On any given day, legislators may have to attend meetings with constituents, committee hearings, floor sessions, rallies, fundraisers, and lobbying events. It is common for them to be so busy that their legislative assistants (LAs) schedule them in fifteen-minute increments. Anything you can do to make it easier for a legislator to get to your panel discussion, like locating it on the capitol campus, increases the likelihood they will be able to attend. If it is difficult to reserve a room at the capitol, you may want to reach out to your representatives and ask for their assistance in booking a room. Their legislative assistant may be able to help you access rooms that are not available to the general public. Keep in mind that you will likely need to reserve a room at the capitol months in advance, even if you are working with an LA.

Recruiting legislators to participate in your panel can be difficult. Many of them have incredible pressures on their time. They may be reluctant to commit to an event, especially if you are not their constituent. You should consider the range of possibilities and strategies noted in chapter 2 for making connections with legislators and staff. The following specific strategies can also help with recruiting legislators for your event:

- Begin by inviting your own representatives. As a constituent, you have more leverage when you make the ask. They will want to accommodate your request, if at all possible.
- Ask your legislators to suggest other legislators for the panel. Get their permission to use their names when making asks of their colleagues to join. For example, you might say, "Senator Dziedzic is attending the panel and said you would be a great addition. Would you be willing to join us?"
- Keep in mind that it is easier to ignore a phone call or an email than it is to ignore a person standing in front of you. Bring invitations and a factsheet about your class and deliver them in person to legislators.
- Identify people in your networks who have relationships with legislators and ask them to make an introduction for you. You may know people who volunteered on a legislator's campaign. You may be part of an organization that employs a lobbyist, who can connect you to legislators who would be a good fit. You do not always have to have a personal connection to the legislator, but it helps if you know someone who does.
- Emphasize your desire for partisan and chamber balance in your ask. If you have only been able to get Democrats to agree to speak on the panel, you may be able to get Republicans to commit by noting the disparity. You could say something like, "It's so important to me that there is partisan balance on the panel, but so far only Democrats have agreed to come. Would you be willing to come talk with my students to ensure that the conversation isn't one-sided?" This type of question can also work when recruiting legislators from the House and the Senate. Often, the two bodies have different cultures and priorities. If you have mostly legislators from one chamber, pointing out that imbalance can help you recruit legislators from the other.
- Expect that it will be difficult to recruit and there will be many cancellations. Ask at least twice as many legislators as you hope will attend. Accept that it will likely take multiple calls and emails with LAs to get

your event on legislators' schedules. Plan to send an email to make the initial ask, followed by a call to the LA to check on the status of the request. It is also a good idea to make confirmation calls to LAs a couple of days before the event.

To prepare for the event, you will want to have a document that includes a short introduction for each legislator who may attend. You will likely want to include the following information in their introduction:

· Their party
· Their district number
· The cities in their district
· How many terms they have served in the legislature
· The committees they are on
· Any notable legislation they are the primary author on that session

You may also want to reach out to their LA to see whether there's anything else the legislator would like included in their introduction. It is also a good idea to check with the LA to ensure that you have the correct pronunciation of the legislator's name and their pronouns.

On the day of the event, you will have the opportunity to model adaptability and responsiveness for your students. Although you may schedule your discussion for sixty or ninety minutes, it is unlikely that many of the legislators will be able to join you for the entire time. It's more likely that you will have legislators dropping in to speak with students for fifteen to twenty minutes at a time. As a result, you may want to prepare two sets of questions. The first is a small set of questions that you can ask every legislator. Having a standard set of questions that are answerable in approximately fifteen minutes will make it possible to accommodate those who need to enter and exit quickly. It is also a good idea to have an additional set of questions that you can ask legislators if they are able to stay longer. Lists of possible questions you might ask the legislators are included in a sample question list later in this chapter. Certainly you can and should ask basic biographical and background questions, but this is also an opportunity to engage legislators in questions about norms and participation as noted above.

Students will likely also have questions for the legislators. In general, legislators are most excited about interacting with students and will be particularly keen to answer questions that come from students directly. It is not uncommon for a legislator to arrive and announce they only have ten or fifteen minutes to answer questions, but then stay significantly longer as they get into conversation with students. Your ability to adapt to shifting schedules and unpredictable availability will make this activity more enjoyable and productive.

After the event, it is good practice to send a thank you card to the legislator for attending your class meeting. You might recruit or assign some of your students to this task, as writing personal thank you notes is an important communication skill that you can emphasize. You might write one to model for them. It is also good to send a thank you email to legislative assistants for everything they did to ensure the legislator actually arrived at your event. LAs do an incredible amount of work to manage legislators' schedules, along with all the other important work they do to make the legislator's work at the capitol possible. Thus, it's also important to thank LAs for their work, though you can probably be less formal with LAs and use email, rather than a paper card.

Meeting-Script Assignment

The meeting-script assignment is a vitally important part of preparing students for their advocacy meetings at the capitol. For this assignment, students write a word-for-word script of what they intend to say in their meetings with legislators. The purpose of this assignment is to have students think through the stories they want to share, the facts they want to present, and who will speak during each section of the meeting. To be clear, the expectation is not that students will memorize the script and deliver it exactly in their meetings. Their conversations with legislators will not be so neatly predictable. However, planning a word-for-word script is still an important exercise for students. Doing so ensures they are able to run an effective meeting on a tight timeline while covering the necessary information they need to share.

The meeting script should have the following components:

- The meeting should both begin and end with thanking the legislator for taking the time to meet with students.
- Students should clearly communicate the purpose of the meeting at

the outset. For example, "We're here to discuss HF28, a bill that would restore voting rights to formerly incarcerated people upon their release from prison."

- Each student should be prepared to share a story or a statement about why the bill is important to them. If directly impacted by the bill, students can share how the bill would impact them, their families, and/or their communities.
- Each meeting should include a section in which students inform the legislator about their bill. In this section of the meeting, students should provide background information about the bill and the problem it is meant to solve. They should offer arguments in favor of the bill. Additionally, they should explain the opposition's position and offer a response meant to address the opposition's objections.
- Each meeting should end with a "hard ask," which means that students should ask the legislator to make a commitment to support their bill. A hard ask should be a yes-or-no question. The point is to make the legislator take a position on the bill. If the legislator will not take a position on the bill, a good follow-up question students can ask is, "What additional information would you need to make a decision on this bill?" If possible, the students can then seek out that information and follow up with the legislator later.

Sample assignment guidelines are included later in this chapter.

Elevator Speech Assignment

While students are at the capitol to attend their scheduled meetings with legislators, they will also have the opportunity to speak with others about their bills. They may run into a legislator while exiting a committee meeting or walking across the campus. Often legislators have only a few minutes to share their perspective; when that moment arises, it is critical to be prepared to take advantage of it. The elevator speech assignment prepares students to make the most of these brief encounters at the capitol.

The elevator speech assignment asks students to prepare a short and compelling "pitch" for their bill. Most versions of this assignment honor the idea of a quick elevator ride with an audience and limit the pitch to less than thirty to sixty seconds. Some versions ask students to start with a "hook"—an engaging question that draws the listener into a conversation so that they might launch their pitch. The expectation is that students will memorize the elevator speech and be comfortable enough with it that they can utilize it at a moment's notice.

The elevator speech should include the following components:

- A statement of the problem
- Basic bill information (such as bill number, companion bill)
- How the bill solves the problem
- A hard ask: Typically, "Will you vote for this bill?"

This assignment often allows students to "flex new muscles" by providing an opportunity to practice one-on-one interpersonal communication skills. Sample assignment guidelines for the elevator speech are included later in this chapter.

Public Testimony Assignment

The public testimony assignment offers students the chance to show up and show support for or against a policy. Testimony typically consists of a brief speech before legislators, provided during a special set-aside period of time during committee and subcommittee meetings. Speakers often must sign up ahead of time and are subject to content and time restraints; students and instructors should identify the opportunities and protocols for providing testimony that are relevant to their state legislative context. It is often possible to sign up for alerts for a bill, which will notify you of impending committee meetings and opportunities for testimony.

The most effective testimony is authentic and clear and leaves a lasting impression. In most cases, an advocate can submit written testimony or sign up ahead of time to give oral testimony, either in person or virtually. Guidelines for testimony, particularly when used as a class assignment, are provided later in this chapter.

Meeting/Reflection Journal

Your students should log or otherwise track their advocacy activities. Basic logging of meetings and actions are helpful for you to monitor students and ensure active participation, and it also allows students to keep useful notes and information for later assignments.

There are various methods you can use to track student activity, from using forms and worksheets to shared online documents. You can ask students to log simple meeting logistics in a spreadsheet or develop more of a narrative journal that incorporates some reflection. You can ask students to log group activity or offer more individualized responses to their meetings. Some ENACT instructors even ask students to take pictures and text or otherwise submit them to the instructor in real time, to enable immediate tracking and generate good content for later campus marketing efforts. (Your marketing office may appreciate pictures of students engaged in advocacy work and meeting with state legislators.) Possible guidelines for this assignment are included below.

You can also use tracking assignments to think about how students should spend their time at the capitol. Do you wish to require a certain number of meetings? Or do you want to schedule time at the capitol and let students fill that time as they see fit—or as circumstances allow? On this latter point, it is again helpful for you to model adaptability for students; a carefully scheduled day of meetings may be scrambled at any point due to legislators' availability.

Additional Resources

Class Readings

Discussions of representation, identity, and class may seem difficult for you to start if you are not currently engaged in such work in your current courses. Still, there are a number of resources from the literature that can help you start classroom discussions that can then be connected to what is happening in your state legislature. A few of these include:

- Alan Rosenthal's *Engines of Democracy*.[2] Although written in 2009, Rosenthal's *Engines of Democracy* is still an excellent choice of primary textbook for the course. The second and third chapters, "The Lives of Legislators" and "Rooted in Their Districts," offer students important insights into why people run for state office and what it means to represent their constituents. Students often begin the course with many negative associations with politicians, much of it attributable to media coverage of national politics and political scandals. These chapters humanize legislators and give students a better understanding of the sacrifices state legislators make when they serve. The framework Rosenthal develops for discussing legislators' motivations and relationships with their constituents can be easily drawn upon when developing questions for legislators for the panel discussion with legislators activity.

- *Beth Reingold's "Gender, Race/Ethnicity, and Representation in State Legislatures."*[3] As discussed above, it is important for students to have the opportunity to reflect on descriptive representation at their state legislature. Understanding who is present, who is absent, and the factors that lead some groups to be overrepresented while others are underrepresented is an important part of developing the capacity to evaluate the representativeness of our institutions and the possibility of democracy. Beth Reingold's article is a great resource for students beginning to explore these questions. Reingold discusses the demographic changes in state legislatures since the Voting Rights Act, as well as the relationship between electoral institutions and increased representation for nondominant groups. This short article provides a good starting point for important conversations about descriptive representation and community power.
- Sayu Bhojwani's *People Like Us: The New Wave of Candidates Knocking at Democracy's Door.*[4] It is important for students to understand the ways economic class influences who gets to run for and hold office. Working-class people face a number of structural and interpersonal barriers when running for office that makes it less likely for them to be recruited, to run, and to win. As a result, our state legislators tend to come from more privileged economic backgrounds. In the chapter, "The Cost of Public Life," Sayu Bhojwani tells the stories of low-income immigrant elected officials and the challenges they faced running for office and serving due to class and race. This chapter does an excellent job of connecting institutions to personal experiences, making it easy for students to understand how institutional design choices impact who runs, who wins, and who gets represented in our state legislatures.
- *Resource Generation's "Class Distinctions and Income Brackets."*[5] It has become common for universities to encourage or even require students to take courses focused on racism and sexism. Discussions of class and classism are far less common. Students, like people in the United

States generally, often struggle to identify their own economic class and fail to appreciate the ways in which class influences our perspectives and experiences. Resource Generation, a progressive organization that focuses on redistributing wealth from the top 10% of the economic distribution to movement organizations that represent lower income people, the working class, and other marginalized people, has developed an online resource that can offer a helpful starting point for understanding the significance of class in our lives. The online resource, "Class Distinctions and Income Brackets," describes common life circumstances experienced by members of different classes, as well as the percentage of total US wealth that is held by each group. This can be a helpful tool for students working to identify their class location.

- Barbara Jensen's *Reading Classes: On Culture and Classism in America.*[6] Faculty looking for a longer-form exploration of class, classism, and personal identity may enjoy Barbara Jensen's *Reading Classes*. In this memoir, Jensen discusses her personal experience of class mobility—from working class to middle class—while offering an account of class cultures and the stigma working-class and people living in poverty face in our society. While her story focuses on the ways in which working-class students are misread, demeaned, and ignored in educational institutions, the experiences she describes are directly translatable to other institutions that primarily reflect middle- and upper-class cultural values, like state legislatures. This book offers faculty and students an excellent starting point for important conversations about class and classism in all our institutions.

These readings can open up the possibilities for other sources from the literature that may fit your state and local circumstances even more than these.

Elevator Pitch Models

There are considerable resources available in the business studies literature, as well as online, for "pitching" ideas. Many of these sources are well-suited and translatable to the political context and might be helpful for you in preparing that assignment. For example, many ENACT instructors have relied upon the EPIC "laser talk" model developed by the nonprofit advocacy organization RESULTS.[7] (EPIC stands for Engage, state the Problem, Inform about the solution, and Call to action.)

Conclusion

Direct, engaged conversations with legislators are in many ways the heart of the ENACT experience. The assignments described in this chapter are designed to provide students with the skills and tools necessary to make that experience successful and lower any anxiety or concern they may have about those meetings. Note also that these assignments, while designed to build arguments and resources for meeting legislators, are often helpful for, and overlap with, communication with the public that is often also part of legislative advocacy. (See chapter 5.)

Still, you may have some concerns about feasibility for your particular situation. Again, you may have some resource or logistical constraints that prevent you from scheduling multiple visits to the capitol. And as we pointed out in chapter 1, your college calendar may not align perfectly with the legislative session, especially in states with part-time legislators. Still, even if these logistical constraints limit your possibilities, you can still maximize your students' encounters in the "halls of power," while also demystifying and contextualizing those institutional settings. The alternative tour of the capitol does not require a legislature to be in session, and a meeting with a legislator in their local constituency office outside of session still allows at least some discussion of institutional norms and representation, not to mention advocacy work.

No matter when they meet legislators and staffers, students are often heartened, even amazed, by how much they show an interest in the students and their work. While not every legislative meeting is positive, the vast majority are. You can help students contribute to the best possible outcome for these meetings by ensuring they are well prepared through these assignments.

> *The Advocacy for Policy Change class showed me that contacting and conversing with legislators is possible. This made my effort feel worthwhile, which encouraged me to continue to engage in a number of small ways.*
>
> —from a survey of Brandeis alumni who participated in ENACT course

Sample Capitol Tour Activity

After many hours of learning about the art and architecture of the state capitol, Dr. Kathleen Cole, ENACT fellow in Minnesota, found that the narrative expressed there is a celebration of settler colonialism and the "great men" of Minnesota history. Much of the artwork on the capitol campus uses symbolism to praise settlers and offer justifications for western expansion and land theft. One of the most famous works—which is used as the front-page image on the legislature's website—is a statuary called *The Progress of the State.* In this statuary, four horses pull a chariot containing a white man. The horses are meant to represent the natural elements: earth, air, fire, and water. Between the horses stand two white women, meant to represent agriculture and industry. The white man in the chariot is meant to symbolize Minnesota itself. He stands in the chariot, while the animals and women stand on the ground. His position is meant to evoke his mastery over "nature (the horses) and civilization (the women)" and serve as an "allegory . . . in which mankind proceeds toward prosperity without fear."[8]

A similar perspective is expressed throughout the murals inside the building and is especially evident in the murals that surround the rotunda. These four murals are collectively titled *Civilization of the Northwest.* The murals tell the story of a white man whom, according to the Minnesota Historical Society, the artist referred to as "American Genius." He sets off on his "civilizing" journey after being blessed by women meant to represent hope and wisdom in the first panel. In the second panel, he "scourges the west of its noncivilizing features," including "savagery . . . cowardice . . . sin . . . [and] stupidity."[9] In the next panel, he "rips stones from the soil and releases wealth and fertility."[10] In the final panel, the white man sits on a throne and "directs the four winds to carry out his will."[11] This set of murals presents a common settler colonialist narrative of "expansion"—or what might more accurately be described as dispossession or land theft. In the murals, the original inhabitants of the land are unrepresented. Instead, the white settler comes upon wild, uncivilized, uninhabited land and through his mighty efforts makes the land civilized through extracting resources from it and making it thereby productive and profitable. The erasure of the original inhabitants of this land—the Dakota and Anishinaabe peoples—is an important absence in the story, one that allows the allegory to glorify, rather than condemn, "American Genius."

In other capitol murals, Native American people are simultaneously present in the image, yet conceptually erased through the titles and meanings of the paintings. For example, in the senate chamber, you'll find the mural *Discoverers and Civilizers Led to the Source of the Mississippi.* In the painting, a large group of white "explorers" are led to the headwaters of the Mississippi River by the "Spirit of Discovery... [and the] Spirit of Civilization," each represented as white women who are winged angels. When the explorers arrive at the source of the river, they find three Native Americans there; however, the presence of Native people does not preclude them from "discovering" the river.

A similar scene occurs in *Father Hennepin Discovering the Falls of St. Anthony.* In the painting, Catholic priest Louis Hennepin stands at the edge of St. Anthony Falls. He holds a cross out toward the water while saying something toward it—maybe a blessing, maybe attempting to claim the location for a colonial power. Sitting at his feet are many Native Americans. To his right, a seminude Native woman carries something toward the group. Again, their presence does not preclude the priest from "discovering" the falls Native people had lived near for hundreds, if not thousands, of years.

Another theme in the artwork at the Minnesota capitol is the "great men" of Minnesota history. In the rotunda, visitors will find statues of Minnesotans who served in the Civil War. Throughout the hallways are portraits and busts of Minnesota governors. All these artworks represent white men. Indeed, white men are the protagonists in the narrative of Minnesota that is established through the art throughout the capitol campus. The story of the state, as told in the paintings and statuary, is the story of white men taming wild lands, bringing civilization westward, winning battles, and ruling Minnesota. To the extent that other people are represented in the artwork they are background characters, present to witness or bless the greatness of white men.

When Dr. Cole does the capitol tour activity with students, she gives them the same questions about the art and architecture listed in the description of the assignment earlier in the chapter. Students have time to explore the capitol grounds on their own to inspect the art prior to the tour beginning. Once the tour begins, she takes her students to the house chamber, the senate chamber, the supreme court chamber, and the governor's office. At each of these locations, students can view the artworks as well as photographs of all the government officials serving in each chamber. This gives students the opportunity to notice the demographic makeup of the government, while thinking critically about the narrative constructed by the building.

Sample Questions for Panel Discussion with Legislators

Below are two lists of questions you may consider asking legislators at the panel event.

The short list:

- Can you talk a little bit about your district? Who are your constituents? What are the political issues that matter most to the people you represent?
- What does it mean to you to represent your community? How do you understand the relationship between you as a representative and your constituents? Are there other groups besides constituents from your district you feel you represent at the capitol?
- What are your legislative priorities this session?

The longer list:

- What was your life like before becoming a legislator? And why did you get involved in politics? What made you decide to run for office?
- How do you balance your legislative responsibilities with your other responsibilities like outside work and family obligations?
- What are the political issues that are most important to you and drive your work?
- It's common to hear about the importance of norms of civility and reciprocity for interactions between legislators—especially between those on opposing sides of the issues. How important are norms of civility and reciprocity for your work? As those norms have eroded in political discourse, have you seen an effect on the way in which legislators treat each other?
- What makes a good meeting or a bad meeting with a constituent? From a legislator's perspective, what are the components of an effective meeting?

- You have so many people who are trying to influence the way you vote in the legislature. What kind of communications are most likely to impact your thinking on a political issue? What kind of information do you need? What method of contact is most impactful?
- Majority parties and minority parties must use power differently in the legislature. When your party is in the majority, how do you use power? If you're in the minority, what are the different strategies you use for leveraging power?

Sample Assignment Guidelines for Meeting Script

Assignment. For this script assignment, you need to write out word for word everything you plan to say during your meeting with the legislator, indicating who on your team will make each point you need to say.

Your meeting script is part script, part agenda that you will prepare in advance of meeting with legislators. You should plan for your meeting with the legislator to last no more than fifteen minutes. So, it's important that you are prepared and focused so that you can get through all the points you need to make.

A good script will have the following components:

- It should both begin and end with thanking the legislator for taking the time to meet with you.
- You should clearly communicate at the outset the purpose of your meeting.
- You should prepare a statement about why this issue is important to you.
- You should inform the legislator about your bill, providing background information, your arguments in favor/against the bill, your opposition's view, and your response to the opposition's view.
- The ask: What is it that you want your legislator to do? Be direct and specific.

When writing your script, be sure to assign speaking tasks to everyone in the group equitably. Also, be sure to plan and indicate in your script how much time each part of the meeting will take.

Sample Assignment Guidelines for Elevator Speech

Assignment. An elevator speech or pitch is a very brief speech that quickly introduces your listener to your issue. It is called an elevator speech because you're supposed to be able to make your point in the amount of time that it takes to ride the elevator with someone for a few floors. Your elevator speech assignment should be less than thirty seconds in length, without rushing through your speaking.

Your elevator speech assignment should include the following parts:

- A "hook" or engaging question that starts the conversation (optional)
- A statement of the problem
- Basic bill information (i.e., bill number, companion bill, short description of the goal of the bill)
- Does the bill solve the problem you have identified or make it worse?
- The ask: What action do you want the legislator to take?

Sample Elevator Speech

Optional hook: When is the last time you took an Uber somewhere? or, How often do you use rideshares?

Huge corporations like Uber and Lyft are able to skirt minimum wage laws by improperly categorizing their drivers as independent contractors. As a result, rideshare drivers often end up making less than minimum wage. These exploitative wages disproportionately harm immigrants and communities of color. HF2369 is a bill before the House that would solve this problem by mandating wages for rideshare drivers that meet minimum wage requirements. Can we count on you to support HF2369?

Sample Assignment Guidelines for Public Testimony

Assignment: Some legislative sessions include time for the public to offer their thoughts about a bill. You will prepare a brief statement in support of your chosen bill. Below are some suggested steps to take in order to prepare and deliver your testimony.

How to prepare your testimony:

- Prepare your comments in advance.
- Include the full bill name and number.
- Do your homework and address the committee formally, using their titles.
- Include your name and where you live.
- You may choose to share your title/occupation if it lends expertise, but you do not need to be an expert to be heard or taken seriously. You are a citizen and, therefore, your opinion matters. We all wear different hats. Sometimes sharing about yourself can help the legislator categorize you (mother, father, grandmother, small business owner, teacher, school board member, community volunteer, healthcare worker, religious leader, community organizer, student). Not to sound too cynical, but politicians want votes. They want to know what types of people are interested in different policies. Help them make those connections. If everyone introduces themselves as an "environmentalist" when giving testimony on an environmental bill, for example, it does not really help a legislator see all the other communities they are a part of.
- If you are officially representing a group, share the name of that group and whom that group serves.
- Make very clear whether you are asking legislators to support or oppose the bill. If you are recommending modifications, make that clear and include those changes in your written testimony.
- Stick to the time constraints of the hearing. This is typically three minutes; find out ahead of time. The only way to effectively present your message in the given time is by practicing and timing yourself until it is right.
- End it with a bang: one sentence that crystallizes your point and how they should vote.
- Thank them for their time.

Other things to keep in mind:

- Different messages appeal to different people. Some people are swayed by facts and figures, others by human storytelling. Think about what kind of message you want to share. What is most authentic to you?
- Just as when writing an op-ed, make one point and make it well. Issues are complex and often there are many angles; you should focus on one if

you want to make impactful testimony. You do not have to tell the whole story. This is where working with collaborators can be helpful—divide and conquer the different parts of the issue.

- You may choose to go with a personal story. How does this connect personally with you? What story can help them see how this is important to you and other voters like you? How can your story clarify the stakeholders and the stakes? Who is negatively affected if things do not change? Who will benefit if things do change? How can your storytelling paint a picture that makes an impression?
- You may choose to go with facts. If so, make sure your facts are from legitimate sources, not just from the internet. Use reputable scientific sources and share the source of your data. A little data or a few statistics can go a long way. Select the data points that are most useful to the story you are telling, and work to craft data or statistics into digestible sound bites. What can people easily remember? What helps them visualize the problem?

How and whether to handle questions:

- At the end of your testimony, legislators may ask you questions. Whether you want to answer them is up to you. If you feel like an expert, do it. If you are not good with off-the-cuff speaking, you may choose not to ask for questions. Your response to a question will likely be the final impression you leave, so be certain you are prepared and will end strongly.
- If you want to take questions, first brainstorm, based on your testimony, what kinds of questions they might ask you. Ask friends to read your proposed comments and share potential questions with you.
- Just like you might practice for a job interview, practice responses to the questions you think you are most likely to hear.

Follow-up is vital. No matter how you share your opinions with policymakers and leaders, following up can help them understand that you are paying attention to them and the actions they are taking. Also share your testimony with your own legislators, even if they are not on the committee.

Sample Assignment Guidelines for Meeting/Reflection Journal

Group Meeting Log

Assignment. For each of your meetings with legislators, committee hearing, meeting with advocacy coalitions, or other advocacy campaign activity, please log the following:

- Description of meeting ("advocacy visit with legislator," "meeting with advocacy group," "public hearing," etc.)
- Date and time of meeting, approximately how long it lasted, and modality (in person, Zoom, etc.)
- Name(s) of meeting attendees (if a committee hearing, just the name of the committee and chair)
- Brief description of the meeting, your group's level of participation (active participants or observers), and a general overview of how it went (~150 words)

Individual Reflection

For at least *two* of the meetings described above, *each* member of the group should post an individual journal entry of approximate 250 words. In your entry, you should address some or all of the following questions:

- What went well in the meeting? What might have worked better?
- Did you and/or your group make any connections with individuals at the meeting?
- What were your general impressions of the people you met with?
- Was there anything about the meeting that surprised you?
- How does this meeting connect to the materials we've looked at in class?

NOTES

1. Dana Ferguson, "'Opportunity to Make History': Communities of Color Look to Lawmakers to Close Gaps," MPR News, February 13, 2023, www.mprnews.org/story/2023/02/13/opportunity-to-make-history-communities-of-color-look-to-lawmakers-to-close-gaps; Sam Stroozas, "'Shaking Things Up': Minnesota's LGBTQ Lawmakers See New

Strength at Capitol," MPR News, January 17, 2023, www.mprnews.org/story/2023/01/17/were-shaking-things-up-minnesotas-lgbtq-lawmakers-see-new-strength-at-capitol.

2. Alan Rosenthal, *Engines of Democracy: Politics and Policymaking in State Legislatures* (Washington, DC: CQ Press, 2009).

3. Beth Reingold, "Gender, Race/Ethnicity, and Representation in State Legislatures," *PS: Political Science & Politics* 52, no. 3 (2019): 426–29.

4. Sayu Bhojwani, *People Like Us: The New Wave of Candidates Knocking at Democracy's Door* (New York: The New Press, 2018).

5. "Class Distinctions & Income Brackets," Resource Generation, accessed July 1, 2024, https://resourcegeneration.org/breakdown-of-class-characteristics-income-brackets.

6. Barbara Jensen, *Reading Classes: On Culture and Classism in America* (Ithaca, NY: ILR Press, 2012).

7. "Tool: Laser Talk," *The Leading Teacher*, Fall 2012, https://learningforward.org/wp-content/uploads/2012/08/tools-laser-talks.pdf.

8. Neil B. Thompson, *Minnesota's State Capitol: The Art and Politics of a Public Building* (St. Paul: Minnesota Historical Society Press, 1974), 56.

9. Ibid., 68.

10. Ibid.

11. Ibid.

5

Engaging with the Public

SUCCESS AT THE CAPITOL depends on more than just persuasive meetings with legislators. It also often depends on the ability to win support from the public. In this chapter, we discuss strategies for effectively engaging with legislators and the public. When engaging in advocacy work, it is important to consider how actions connect to—or fail to connect to—a range of people. The actions that connect to political decision-makers and decision-making are direct and impactful. That said, garnering support from the public can amplify your effect by encouraging others to communicate their political needs to leaders.

This chapter also includes student assignments, such as the policy brief and op-ed submissions. We provide tips and suggestions about tools that may not be part of a formal class assignment but may allow students to engage peers and community members in supporting their advocacy work. These are valuable topics to explore in class discussions and include strategies like engaging through the arts, sharing with community groups, and using social media. We provide guidance for involving local opinion editors, artists/activists, and policy specialists as guest speakers to prepare students to develop impactful public arguments.

Key Questions

Who else is working on your students' chosen issues?

While enthusiasm for an issue is a wonderful thing, an important part of understanding a problem or an issue is learning about the organizations working on the topic. Students should research nonprofits in the state to learn about groups that might be advocating for their issue. Students might first believe that an advocacy group for a given sector will be advocating for all policies on that issue in a given session. They might be surprised to find that, for example, a prominent state environmental group is not interested in promoting a particular environmental bill during the session.

It is important to help students understand the broad, incremental, multiyear approach that many advocacy organizations must take. An advocacy group may have been following the students' selected bill, or another version of it, as it has slowly worked its way through the legislature over many years. Advocacy groups may decide to support a less stringent policy with a higher potential for success with the intention of using it as a gateway to stronger policy in the future. Advocacy groups may have to make tough decisions on where to concentrate their resources. They may have to choose one or two policies on which to focus their efforts in a given session, at the expense of any work on other bills. Any successful advocacy organization likely has a multiyear plan for the issues that are important to them.

As such, students are advised to reach out to organizations and make a connection, while also recognizing that the people who work at advocacy organizations are often very busy during any legislative session. A student can share that they will be working on a given policy, leaving an invitation open for the group to contact them if they would like to collaborate. A sample email is included later in this chapter.

While it is not necessary that students only work on bills important to advocacy groups in the field, they can learn a great deal, build bridges, and grow their network by sharing information with these groups and learning what they have planned for the legislative session. By coordinating with an organization, students may be able to amplify the organization's impact. Passing or stopping legislation can be more successful when a broad coalition works together. Working with others has the added benefit of amplifying the students' impact, too. When students learn about the stakeholders and organizations working on issues that are important to them, it can also be an important component of their professional development. These kinds of collaborations can lead to internships, job opportunities, and the chance to explore careers students had not yet considered.

> *Even while taking this class online during the Covid-19 pandemic, I appreciated the approach the class took toward teaching students about the legislative process of how bills turn into law. I found it interesting to research the issue of menstrual equity...as well as learning about the issues that other students from the class were researching for the bills they were advocating for that semester. This allowed me to see how policy is intertwined [with] other academic disciplines, such as sociology, politics, public health, etc.*
>
> Alison Cantor, Brandeis University

What kinds of public communication and engagement work best, and in which contexts?

Another important consideration when embarking on advocacy with the public is that different forms of outreach will speak to different communities and constituencies. For some, the expert data, statistics, and facts from a policy brief will be most convincing. For others, an economic argument will be most persuasive. For still others, the storybooks or storycards that emphasize personal stories of regular people in the community can help them realize how many different types of people will be affected by a policy. A range of approaches can help students understand that not all communication connects with people in the same way and that part of successful advocacy might be connecting the right information with the right person. What is also true is that a student may not understand what kind of message connects with the public or with a given legislator until they are in the moment, sharing material that either connects or doesn't. As such, you should seek as much as possible to introduce students to a diversity of approaches and messaging so that they have a toolbox of strategies for engagement.

Assignments and Other Key Course Components

While in this volume we break down the ENACT approach into different components, it is important to remember that many of these components are interrelated. And so, the public-facing materials and assignments described in this chapter are related to—and in some ENACT course models, assigned alongside—the legislative research assignments and elevator speech outlined in chapters 3–4.

Policy Brief

A policy brief is a way to share well-researched, clear, persuasive information that compellingly demonstrates why an issue is important and links it to policy solutions. The audience for a policy brief is wider than just the legislative research report and one-pager described in chapter 3, although certainly some readers may be the legislators themselves. Still, this brief is also designed to be offered to politically engaged members of the general public.

It is important that a brief is just that: brief! The policy brief can be shared with policymakers at the statehouse and other important stakeholders. Politicians and others are busy people and are unlikely to read a long or wordy document. And yet, it is important to produce something that has legitimate sources and is based on solid scientific data. So, while it is "brief," it must be very carefully researched. The style used in a policy brief is also important; the most compelling writing does not try to tell the reader how to think or what to do. Instead, persuasive writing shares powerful facts that cannot be denied—in essence, flooding the reader with evidence that they must consider.

A policy brief is research-focused and may serve as an alternative to traditional research paper assignments. Again, it may serve as either an alternative or a companion to the legislative research report described in chapter 3. Many of the same components of a research paper, including using and properly citing literature from peer-reviewed sources, summarizing and synthesizing research, and cohesive writing, will be parts of a strong policy brief.

Still, for your students, the policy brief can feel like a different type of writing assignment, one that asks them to flex muscles they may not be using in other writing. It must pack a great deal of information into a short document but also be easier to read and more inviting to a general audience than an academic research paper. Sample guidelines are provided below.

Op-ed

"Op-ed" is short for "opposite the editorial page," but is sometimes thought of as an "opinion editorial." This short assignment is another way of advocating for a bill or an issue to the public at large. This essay, typically sent to a print or online newspaper, provides an opportunity to sway public opinion about an issue by sharing facts and personal experiences. As a course assignment, op-eds feature concise and persuasive writing; they allow students to distill all they have learned about their issue into one short-form piece. Writing an op-ed demands that the author write very clearly and compellingly, and these are excellent skills to nurture in students. Assignment guidelines are included at the end of this chapter. Because this is an unusually public-facing assignment with particular format needs, we have also included a grading rubric for guidance to instructors.

You should consider whether you have options for publication of this assignment in your state context. As noted earlier, "news deserts" proliferate in some capital cities and states, and so you may have limited options for a newspaper to place a student op-ed. Some ENACT instructors prefer to format the op-ed as a letter to the editor instead; these letters are often seen as less authoritative opinions of "regular citizens" and so may offer more access and possibility for publication. Still, you might look for alternative placements; local bloggers or newsletters, online news sources, or even your campus student newspaper can offer a chance for your students to actually share their arguments with the public.

> *I write comment letters and op-eds and participate in legislative meetings as part of my job. The Advocacy for Policy Change [course] gave me the tools to come into the job prepared.*
>
> —from a survey of Brandeis alumni who participated in ENACT course

Social Media

Social media has the potential to connect with a much larger audience than you could ever reach in one-on-one advocacy. It can allow you to connect with others doing similar or the same work in your community and around the world. Social media outreach can allow you to amplify voices that are not often heard or centered when considering an issue. The downside of social media outreach is that it may not connect with political decision-making or political decision-makers. Social media can be an echo chamber of like-minded people. That can be wonderful when you are looking for confirmation but may not lead to any political impact.

The most productive way to use social media in advocacy is to connect it to events and activities that have bearing on political decision-making. Below we share brief information about different kinds of social media and hints on using them for advocacy work; later in the chapter we offer sample guidelines for a video assignment that can also be connected to social media platforms.

- *Facebook* can be a good way to connect with community organizations and find others working on issues in your community, particularly advocates who are not associated with a formal nonprofit organization. Facebook can be used to build support for local events and connect with a broad network internationally. As a social media platform, it skews older; you are unlikely to connect with young people on Facebook.
- *Instagram* centers images and photos. It can be a fruitful way to share compelling images that can help people understand a problem and how to change it. It can also offer a way to get inspired by people working on issues around the world. Using hashtags can allow your posts to be seen by a wider audience. Most social issues have a wide range of advocates already on this platform. Finding them and following them may grow your network.
- *X (formerly Twitter)* is best suited to pithy comments and breaking news. It can be a great way to find information and connect with a broad network of like-minded individuals. As is the case with Instagram, using keywords in hashtags can help others find your work. Searching with hashtags can help you create a network on the platform.
- *TikTok* should not be underestimated; it is not all dancing. TikTok can connect you with a robust network of people of all ages who want information about a topic, want to share hints and tips, and want to bolster the work of others. There are really vibrant networks of activists working on every issue on TikTok. As is the case with Instagram and X, using hashtags can help you find other activists and enable them to find your

work. A TikTok video might also be used as an assignment. Students can create videos to inform the public about the issue or encourage advocacy on a bill. Using the creation of a TikTok video, or a video for broader or other platforms, as an assignment can also help connect students with other advocates.

However, if you include any social media activities in your ENACT class, be aware of resource differences among students in your group, and don't assume that every student is a "digital native." You should ensure that there is a comfort level with the technical process of producing video among your students and that everyone has access to phone cameras, cloud storage, and editing apps. You might consult with faculty in your communication studies and creative arts departments for resources and technical support.

As always, there is at least some risk involved to students if they share anything publicly on their social media feeds. You might review all videos before letting students publish them and consider whether you will require public sharing as part of the assignment.

Sharing with Community Groups

When advocating for an issue, it may be helpful to think outside the box and connect with new groups. A broad coalition may help legislators see the many different types of people who may be affected—positively or negatively—by a bill. Students can share information about their issue with a wide range of people by reaching out to community groups, libraries, elder care communities, and classrooms ranging from elementary school to college level.

One way of getting the word out about any issue is to simply contact these institutions and ask to share about the policy issue. If you do a good job, the people in these groups will tell others and opportunities for advocacy will expand. To ensure success in sharing an issue with community groups:

- Scaffold your students, either with a formal assignment or more informal mentoring, to bring a compelling presentation that speaks to the audience.
- Have your students confirm how long their presentation should be and

help them alter it to fit the event. Provide time for students to practice their presentation to be certain it meets the time constraints and expectations.
- Older adults will not want to see the same presentation that third graders will enjoy and vice versa. Encourage students to craft a message that is appropriate for the audience.
- Just like when speaking with politicians, students should give people ideas about what to do to solve the problem. Remind them that it is helpful to provide examples of personal things others can do (behavior change) and larger acts (contacting politicians and other leaders).

Additional Resources

Engaging the Public through the Arts

Engaging through the arts can be a powerful tool for advocacy. If pressed, you might not at first be able to recall instances of art-based advocacy, but powerful images and projects have shaped American politics and policy for generations. For example, consider the stylized posters that were a product of the Works Project Administration promoting things as varied as eating vegetables and visiting libraries, or the impact of the Vietnam War Memorial by Maya Lin. Consider the impression made by the AIDS quilt displayed on the National Mall in 1987 or, more recently, think of widely shared videos, photos, memes, lists of names, and other images that have powerfully promoted the Black Lives Matter movement. The arts can reach audiences that cannot be reached in other ways and may leave a lasting impression that cannot be matched by the impression one gains from statistics or data.

The arts can also be used to share data or statistics in more easily understandable forms. They can help communities visualize the scale of a problem. The guiding principles you would use for other types of outreach or communication are also important to use for arts-based engagement. The arts can be used to tell a story, but make sure it is the story you want to tell. Just as would be the case for an op-ed, you want your students' arts engagement to focus on one clear message.

For example, one of the authors, Katharine Owens, has been creating life-size portraits of animals harmed by plastic debris by hand-sewing unrecyclable film plastics onto canvas, a multiyear project called Entangled and Ingested. There are many stories to tell about plastic pollution. There are many policies that have been proposed to combat plastic pollution. A piece of artwork that emphasizes film plastics will not be the best tool to advocate for policies about plastic bottle recycling, for example. It would not be the best tool to pinpoint the health impacts of plastic production on communities. However, it can be a powerful tool to highlight issues of communities' inability to keep up with mounting municipal waste, the impact of plastic waste on animals, or a lack of true recycling options.

The advantages of arts-based approaches are the lasting visual impression that stay with any viewers, the way co-creation of an arts piece can build community and bring groups together in collaboration, the way it can engage audiences of all ages and allows for hopeful engagement, and its creativity and uniqueness, which may allow it to garner media coverage and attention.

How can you use the arts to engage in a policy issue if you are not an artist? Just as you might connect with an expert in policy, you can use campus, community, and online resources to find people advocating on a given issue through the arts. As resources and logistics allow, you can invite them to share their work with your students or to collaborate, depending on your needs and goals for the semester.

Bringing the World to Your Classroom

Do not be afraid to invite experts to share their experience with you in the classroom. Thanks to online platforms like Zoom and Teams, we can infuse classes with information right from the source, in a way that is less time-consuming for the experts and resource-intensive for you. Not everyone will have an interest or the time, but it never hurts to ask. You can invite a wide range of people to share with your students. We have already mentioned a number of these resources and individuals, but you should consider expanding the scope of possible experts to include those outside of your local context if the need arises. Newspaper editors, legislators, artist activists, policy specialists, lobbyists, public relations experts, and artists may have unique insights on how to prepare students to develop impactful public arguments on their chosen bills. If you do invite guest speakers, have students research the guest ahead of time and prepare at least one question for the experts. Use the time of experts wisely and be certain to thank them for their contribution to your class.

Conclusion

Not every ENACT course will have the space and time available for incorporating outreach to the public. Still, teaching students strategies to advocate more broadly in their communities develops skills that reach far beyond the classroom. By working within their communities to build support for the issues that are important to them, students can not only develop a powerful arsenal of communication strategies but also enhance their civic engagement and political efficacy.

Sample Email for Students Contacting Advocacy Groups

Dear Environmental Advocacy Group,

Hi, my name is Katharine Owens and I am a student at the University of Hartford. This year, my American Public Policy class is studying and advocating for bills in the Connecticut General Assembly. I will be advocating for House Bill 1: An Act to Ban Plastic Bags. During this semester-long course, I will be writing a policy brief and an op-ed and sharing stories of people impacted by the bill on my social media accounts. I also plan to visit the capitol to speak with legislators about voting for the bill.

I want you to be aware of the work I plan to do. Please let me know if there is any potential for coordination with any efforts your group may be making to advocate for this bill this session. I realize that you are busy; I simply wanted to share this with you in case it is helpful. Thanks!

Sincerely,
Katharine Owens
ko@university.edu

Sample Assignment Guidelines for Policy Brief

Assignment. Write a short policy brief that makes a succinct case for your position on your chosen bill.

Your brief should include the following substantive sections:

- *Problem Definition.* What is the issue in question? Hint: This is what the policy will fix. Put this problem in your own words.
- *Solution/Policy Recommendations.* What policies address this issue? What have other communities done? What were the impacts? Are there local, state, or national policies that purport to address this issue, even partially?
- *Sources* (to show your brief is well researched). Why is the problem a problem? Your brief will need to convince us with evidence from reliable sources and make a compelling case. Use resources in our library and tools including Google Scholar to find relevant peer-reviewed scientific studies.

Some reminders:

- Keep it brief! Three to five pages maximum.
- Help the reader understand why they should care about the issue.
- Provide example policy solutions to the problem.
- Make certain to use peer-reviewed scientific sources.
- Use bullet points, graphs, and bold text to grab the reader's attention.
- Emphasize the "takeaway" message—politicians and advocates like to communicate in sound bites, so highlight this information.
- Make it jargon-free and easy to understand.
- Consider your audience. Your brief will be written for a specific audience, namely state legislators. Think about how they access information. They are busy people who want facts. They also represent people and want to support policies that will help them get reelected. How is this problem a problem for *them and for their constituents*? What should you emphasize in your writing to capture this audience?

Policy Brief Elements

Title: Create a dynamic title for your policy brief that grabs the reader's attention.

Authors: Include the names of authors who have cowritten the brief.

Define the Problem: This is a paragraph or several paragraphs that will be similar to a literature review, in that they are comprehensive and include references to many peer-reviewed sources that help define the problem. We emphasize peer-reviewed sources, but this section may also include some reports from government, nonprofit, or NGO websites or publications, particularly if they have relevant data about the issue in the region or state. This is your opportunity to demonstrate that the problem is important not because you think it is, but because experts have said many times and in many ways that this issue deserves attention.

Think about what compels people. Is it data about the social costs of a problem? The financial costs of a problem? The answer, of course, is that different ideas motivate different people. Therefore, it is likely more compelling to include a range of types of data. You might use subheadings, bullets, or other strategies to emphasize or draw the eye to the most important takeaway messages. Remember, this will be shared with busy people who may review it briefly before deciding to engage further.

Policy Solutions: This is your opportunity to make the connection between the problem you have defined and policy solutions. This section may focus on the bill being followed in the session. How will the proposed bill make the problem worse or better? If this bill will worsen the problem, are there examples from other states that could improve it? Perhaps the bill is a step in the right direction, but only offers a partial solution. What types of additions or alterations to the bill could better eliminate the problem? You might have the case of a good bill that addresses the problem. If so, help the reader understand how this bill addresses the most important aspects of the problem and can lead to real change.

Note that not every session will have a proposed bill that addresses the issue. Are there examples of bills from other states or localities that can help the legislators think about the problem in new ways?

[*Authors' Note: If you teach in a political environment where public advocacy is unwelcome or particularly risky, you might have students write about policy solutions more generally and not focus on any currently being debated in the session. For example, in 2015, before joining ENACT, Dr. Owens received a grant from NOAA, the National Oceanic and Atmospheric Administration, entitled* From Shore to Statehouse. *The premise of this grant was that students would collect data about plastic pollution in Connecticut and share the results with state legislators. There is an important rule when using federal funding: it cannot be used to advocate or lobby for policy. As such, we proposed that in the resulting policy brief, we would not advocate for or against any policy. Instead, we described the problem and why it was important and shared a range of policies from around the world that addressed plastic pollution. The resulting report did not grade the policies or make any determination about their comparative value. It did not ask legislators to take any action. No collaboration with advocacy or lobbying groups took place. The report was shared with legislators after the session ended and was not tied to any bill under discussion that session.*]

Conclusion: Write a short summary that includes what you are asking the legislator to do.

Contact information: Include your contact information to allow easy communication and connection.

Sources: Include the peer-reviewed sources that support your arguments in footnotes. While footnotes are not often used in the social sciences, we use them in this format to improve readability for the audience.

Sample Policy Brief

Recycling is not enough—let's solve the issue of plastic bag waste in Connecticut!

by Katharine Owens

The Plastics Problem

Litter is not a new problem, but our reliance on disposable and single-use plastic means that waste accumulates—especially in waterways around the world. In the 1950s only about 5 million tons of plastic were produced each year, but now global markets produce more than 350 million tons each year.[i] Plastic in the ocean is increasing at astounding rates. A study published in 2014 estimates the oceans contain "a minimum of 5.25 trillion particles weighing 268,940 tons."[ii] Scientists find this issue so important that they

i. PlasticsEurope. (2022). Plastics: The facts. Retrieved from https://plasticseurope.org/knowledge-hub/plastics-the-facts-2022.

ii. Eriksen, M., et al. (2014). Plastic pollution in the world's oceans: more than 5 trillion plastic pieces weighing over 250,000 tons afloat at sea. *PloS One*, 9(12), e111913.

have recommended plastic be classified as hazardous waste.[iii] More than twenty years of research has found that increasing plastic manufacturing and use will worsen the condition in global oceans.[iv] The global plastic industry produced 2.18 billion tons of plastic from 2011 to 2017 and is on track to increase the amount produced each year.[v] Unfortunately, we cannot recycle our way out of this problem: 95% of plastic packaging globally is not recycled[vi] and 90.5 % of all plastic ever made has never been recycled.[vii]

Why is plastic pollution in waterways a problem?

While an admittedly useful material, plastics cause problems in the environment.

- *Plastics do not break down quickly.* Plastics comprise about 10% of discarded rubbish but a much higher proportion of marine debris. Plastics are estimated to take from hundreds to thousands of years to break down, but this may vary widely depending on circumstances, such as exposure to wind, air, sunlight, etc.[viii]
- *Plastic debris harms wildlife.* Records of animals becoming trapped in plastic (entanglement) and eating and choking on plastic (ingestion) continue to increase since recordkeeping began. From 1997 to 2015, the number increased from 267 to 557 species globally: 100% of turtle

iii. Rochman, C. M., et al. (2013). Policy: Classify plastic waste as hazardous. *Nature, 494*, 169; Mouat, J., Lozano, R., & Bateson, H. (2010). *Economic impacts of marine litter.* Shetland, Scotland, UK: KIMO.

iv. Azzarello, M. Y., & Van Vleet, E. S. (1987). Marine birds and plastic pollution. *Marine Ecology Progress Series, 37*, 295–303; Gregory, M. R. (2009). Environmental implications of plastic debris in marine settings—entanglement, ingestion, smothering, hangers-on, hitch-hiking and alien invasions. *Philosophical Transactions of the Royal Society B: Biological Science, 364*, 2013–2025.

v. PlasticsEurope. (2018). Plastics: The facts. Retrieved from https://plasticseurope.org/wp-content/uploads/2021/10/2018-Plastics-the-facts.pdf.

vi. Agenda, I. (2016). *The new plastics economy: Rethinking the future of plastics.* Geneva: World Economic Forum, Ellen MacArthur Foundation and McKinsey & Company.

vii. Geyer, R., Jambeck, J. R., & Law, K. L. (2017). Production, use, and fate of all plastics ever made. *Science Advances, 3*(7), e1700782.

viii. Barnes, D. K., Galgani, F., Thompson, R. C., & Barlaz, M. (2009). Accumulation and fragmentation of plastic debris in global environments. *Philosophical Transactions of the Royal Society B: Biological Sciences, 364*(1526), 1985–1998.

species are now affected, as well as 66% of marine mammal species and 50% of seabirds.[ix, x]

- *Plastic debris worsens the issue of invasive species.* Floating plastic can serve as rafts for a range of creatures, which use the material to travel to new ecosystems. More than 350 taxa (including microorganisms, seaweed, and invertebrates) have been recorded rafting or floating on litter in all major global oceans. Invasive species in the United States cost an estimated $120 billion in annual damages.[xi, xii]
- *Plastic debris creates a toxic soup in our oceans.* Marine debris produces a toxic cocktail, including the chemicals from plastics manufacturing and those it absorbs from marine environments. Plastic marine debris is both a physical and a chemical hazard, as animals ingest plastic pieces laden with chemicals. Chemicals are transported through these animals to various environments, impacting more than the species originally in contact with the product. The influx of decomposing plastics and the subsequent leaching of toxic chemicals pose a danger to water quality, wildlife, and human health.[xiii, xiv, xv]

ix. Laist, D. W. (1997). Impacts of marine debris: Entanglement of marine life in marine debris including a comprehensive list of species with entanglement and ingestion records. In J. M. Coe & D. B Rogers (Eds.). *Marine debris: Sources, impacts, and solutions* (pp. 99–139). New York: Springer.

x. Kühn, S., Rebolledo, E. L. B., & van Franeker, J. A. (2015). Deleterious effects of litter on marine life. In M. Bergmann, L. Gutow, & M. Klages (Eds.). *Marine anthropogenic litter* (pp. 75–116). New York: Springer.

xi. Kiessling, T., Gutow, L., & Thiel, M. (2015). Marine litter as habitat and dispersal vector. In M. Bergmann, L. Gutow, & M. Klages (Eds.). *Marine anthropogenic litter* (pp. 141–81). New York: Springer.

xii. USFWS. (2012). The cost of invasive species fact sheet. Retrieved from www.fws.gov.

xiii. Barnes, D. K., Galgani, F., Thompson, R. C., & Barlaz, M. (2009). Accumulation and fragmentation of plastic debris in global environments. *Philosophical Transactions of the Royal Society B: Biological Sciences, 364*(1526), 1985–1998.

xiv. Engler, R. E. (2012). The complex interaction between marine debris and toxic chemicals in the ocean. *Environmental Science & Technology, 46*(22), 12302–12315.

xv. Rochman, C. M. (2015). The complex mixture, fate and toxicity of chemicals associated with plastic debris in the marine environment. In M. Bergmann, L. Gutow, & M. Klages (Eds.). *Marine anthropogenic litter* (pp. 117–40). New York: Springer.

Dirty beaches cost money, clean beaches make money!

The issue of litter and waste in global waterways is not just one of environmental harm; it is also costly to clean up and can have far-reaching impacts.

- A study of 31 California beaches found that reducing pollution by 50% at beaches in Orange County could generate $67 million in benefits to Orange County residents over a 3-month period.[xvi]
- An estimate of the cost of damage due to marine litter across the 21 Pacific Rim economies is €949 million annually (€273 million for the fishing industry, €209 million for the shipping industry, and €467 million for marine tourism).[xvii, xviii]
- Removing marine litter costs United Kingdom ports and harbors the equivalent of $2.7 million per year.[xix]
- A 1989 study demonstrated that on the American East Coast, 45% of commercial fishers dealt with caught propellers, 30% suffered from fouled gear, and 40% experienced cooling systems inhibited by debris.[xx]

Policy Solutions

A recent study from the UK found that through 25 years of monitoring seafloor litter, the only downward trend among all observed debris was for plastic bags, which they attributed to local, state, and national policies

xvi. Leggett, C., Scherer, N., Curry, M., Bailey, R., & Haab, T. (2014). Assessing the economic benefits of reductions in marine debris: A pilot study of beach recreation in Orange County, California. *NOAA Marine Debris Program and Industrial Economics, Incorporated*, pp. 1–45. https://stacks.stanford.edu/file/druid:ks485yz2876/MarineDebrisEconomicStudy.pdf.

xvii. McIlgorm, A., Campbell, H. F., & Rule, M. J. (2011). The economic cost and control of marine debris damage in the Asia-Pacific region. *Ocean & Coastal Management*, 54(9), 643–651.

xviii. Chen, C. L. (2015). Regulation and management of marine litter. In M. Bergmann, L. Gutow, & M. Klages (Eds.). *Marine anthropogenic litter* (pp. 395–428). New York: Springer

xix. Newman, S., Watkins, E., Farmer, A., ten Brink, P., & Schweitzer, J. P. (2015). The economics of marine litter. In M. Bergmann, L. Gutow, & M. Klages (Eds.). *Marine anthropogenic litter* (pp. 367–94). New York: Springer.

xx. Wallace, B. (1989). How much do commercial and recreational fishermen know about marine debris and entanglement? Part 1. In R. S. Shomura & M. L. Godfrey (Eds.). *Proceedings of the Second International Conference on Marine Debris*. April 2–7, Honolulu, HI banning bags.[xxi] Bag banning policies work. We can protect Connecticut's industry, people, and wildlife in the Long Island Sound by banning bags.

Plastic bag bans and related policies, including reductions, limitations, and taxes on bags, can be found across the United States in counties like Cuyahoga (OH); towns such as Malibu (CA), Amesbury, Boston, and Aquinnah (MA), Roanoke (VA), New York (NY), Honolulu (HI), and Austin (TX); in states like California and New Jersey; and in dozens of other communities. Duke University's Nicholas Institute's Plastics Policy Inventory compiles and links to all of these policies.[xxii]

Other approaches involve economic policy instruments and do things like:

- Incentivize industries to use less packaging
- Target waste accumulation (i.e., charge for landfill use)
- Pay individuals to collect litter
- Charge for throwing away litter according to how toxic it is
- Discourage polluting behavior through fines or ticketing[xxiii]

In several countries, fishermen are even paid to collect and return any debris found at sea.[xxiv]

Conclusions

There are a wide range of policy approaches to the issue of plastic pollution. Hundreds of communities around the world have protected their environment and economies by enacting legislation to reduce plastic pollution. We can protect Connecticut's industry, people, and wildlife in the Long

xxi. Maes, T., Barry, J., Leslie, H. A., Vethaak, A. D., Nicolaus, E. E. M., et al. (2018). Below the surface: Twenty-five years of seafloor litter monitoring in coastal seas of North West Europe (1992–2017). *Science of the Total Environment*, 630, 790–98.

xxii. Nicholas Institute for Energy, Environment, and Sustainability. (2024). Plastics policy inventory. Retrieved from https://nicholasinstitute.duke.edu/plastics-policy-inventory.

xxiii. Newman, S., Watkins, E., Farmer, A., ten Brink, P., & Schweitzer, J. P. (2015). The economics of marine litter. In M. Bergmann, L. Gutow, & M. Klages (Eds.) *Marine anthropogenic litter* (pp. 367–94). New York: Springer.

xxiv. Chen, C. L. (2015). Regulation and management of marine litter. In M. Bergmann, L. Gutow, & M. Klages (Eds.). *Marine anthropogenic litter* (pp. 395–428). New York: Springer.

Island Sound by banning bags. Please support House Bill 1: An Act to Ban Plastic Bags.

Please reach out to me if you have any questions.

Katharine Owens, University of Hartford, West Hartford, CT, yourname@emailaddress, (860) 555-1234.

Sample Op-ed Worksheet

Assignment. Produce an op-ed, or opinion piece, that makes a succinct and strong case for your chosen bill. An op-ed is a 600- to 750-word letter to a newspaper where you express an opinion about an issue. It is your job to translate all the things you have learned about your policy issue and your legislation into one short op-ed. This is where all of that knowledge you've accumulated meets the real world.

Questions to keep in mind:

- What is the topic of your op-ed?
- What bill or policy addresses it?
- Is there a timely "hook" (a recent report, a story about this issue in the news, an anniversary of an event, a published article on the topic) that connects with your topic?
- Is there a personal "hook" (does this issue connect to your own life in a meaningful way that you want to share)?
- What newspaper do you want to send your op-ed to—the *New York Times*, the *Washington Post*, *USA Today*, your state flagship paper, your local paper, or something else? Why is your op-ed a good match for that publication?
- What are the requirements for an op-ed submitted to that publication? (How many words? How do they want it submitted?)
- What point do you want to make about this issue?
- What evidence will you use? What would convince people about this issue? What would change their mind?
- What recommendation are you making? What do you want the person who reads this op-ed to do next?
- How would you summarize the point you are trying to make in a few sentences?

Don't forget to:

- Write clearly using accessible language.
- Use short sentences.
- Write several paragraphs; include spaces between paragraphs.
- Make one point clearly and persuasively.
- End with a bang.
- Put your contact information, including name, address, phone, and email at the bottom.

Component	Superlative	Adequate	Inadequate
The problem	Substantive facts about the problem are shared in a way that is compelling and clear.	Facts about the problem are shared, but they are not very compelling or clear.	Few or no facts about the problem are shared.
The solution	The author names the bill and is specific about how the legislation will address the problem (and whether changes are needed).	The author names the bill but does not mention how the legislation will address the problem.	The author does not mention the bill.
Ask	The author mentions the legislation by name and why the public should support or oppose it.	The author either does not mention the legislation by name or does not share why the public should support or oppose it.	The author neither mentions the legislation nor shares why the public should support or oppose it.
General style	Easily readable with short clear sentences and a couple of paragraphs. The author follows the paper's guideline about length.	Not easily readable. Not all sentences are clear. The author follows the paper's guideline about length.	Sentences are long and confusing. The author does not follow the paper's guideline about length.
One main point	The author sticks to one point and emphasizes it throughout the piece.	The author begins with one point, but loses focus at times.	The author does not present one main point.
Contact	The author shares contact information.	The author shares contact information.	The author does not share contact information.

Table 6. Sample Op-ed Grading Rubric.

Sample Assignment Guidelines for Advocacy Video

Assignment. Create a brief "infomercial" video for your bill. Video can be a forum for instant political commentary through such sites as Facebook, TikTok, Instagram, and YouTube. Such videos can be created through original filmmaking or a combination of original footage and existing video clips ("mash-ups-with-messages").

Videos might borrow from the most popular videos, marrying serious substance with lighthearted style. While serious in purpose, video activism can draw on the approach pioneered by entertainment-oriented videos. Short and powerful often can be the best approach, but feel free to be creative; display your group's voice in video.

Your video will be evaluated on its ability to:

- Engage the audience
- Present the problem
- Illustrate a solution
- Call the audience to action
- Create emotional impact
- Display originality

If necessary, remember to identify relevant speakers and cite the source of existing video clips.

6
Life after ENACT

COMPLETING the legislative advocacy project is a huge accomplishment for students. In this chapter, we discuss multiple options for celebrating their accomplishment, as well as what instructors might do to help students consider advocacy and other next steps once they leave the confines of the ENACT classroom.

There are a number of reasons why you should provide some kind of culminating experience as part of the ENACT course. Pedagogical best practices have emphasized culminating projects as important for students in either their entire school career, as in a capstone to a K–12 diploma or undergraduate degree, or on a smaller scale within a single class. End-of-term experiences allow students to combine their skills and knowledge in a tangible way, while also providing the opportunity for them to reflect on their learning. On this latter point, educators in both K–12 and higher education have in recent years emphasized the importance of reflection.[1] Opportunities to reflect on the ENACT experience are particularly important in helping students assess their own future responsibilities, as well as the possibility for future civic engagement, whether professionally or as citizens.

Finally, there is an additional reason why culminating experiences are important—they give students, instructors, and the surrounding community a chance to celebrate their accomplishments. Too often instructors are focused on learning objectives and outcomes, as well as the minutiae of managing a course. Experiential and active learning classes like ENACT bring even more logistical challenges to overcome; you can be forgiven if you end up getting lost in the details. Still, students can find this work exciting, even fun—and it can be rewarding for everyone to bring a spirit of celebration to the end of the course.

This chapter presents options for culminating assignments and activities, as well as some considerations that might lead an educator to choose one type of event over another. We also offer guidance for how to extend students' participation in advocacy work after the course ends, through joining grassroots organizations, becoming members of advocacy organizations, or pursuing work in politics.

> *I am much more confident and assertive when speaking with authority figures. I gained a better understanding of how to advocate for things I care about.*
>
> —from a survey of Brandeis alumni who participated in ENACT course

Key Questions

What is the context of the end of your class?

As noted throughout this volume, the ENACT course is currently being taught across a range of institutions, from community colleges to elite universities, with a variety of practical contexts. For example, some institutions are located near their statehouse; others are geographically isolated. Some states have full-time legislatures with year-round access; other legislatures meet rarely. Similarly, student populations are likewise very diverse. Some of our students with more privileged backgrounds are more likely to feel comfortable interacting with legislators and other professionals at the capitol, while our students who are marginalized due to race, class, gender, citizenship status, or other stigmatized identities may find the capitol grounds unwelcoming, or even hostile, to them.

When choosing culminating events and assignments for the ENACT course, you should take into consideration both the practicalities surrounding the course location and time and the pedagogical and emotional needs of your students. For students who are more likely to feel comfortable at the capitol or come from communities with high rates of civic participation, something like the "present and defend" activity may be the appropriate choice. For students who are more likely to be underrepresented and feel at risk at the capitol, a community celebration event may be a better option.

You should also consider the disciplinary context of your course. Some ENACT courses are focused almost entirely on the ENACT experience; others, however, incorporate an ENACT unit into a disciplinary course. Many of these are based in political science or related social sciences, but as argued throughout this book, the ENACT experience can also be incorporated into a range of disciplines, such as the health sciences and environmental studies. Each disciplinary environment may bring with it different needs for "wrapping up" the course in terms of the goals of the particular program.

Finally, you might consider how "public" the course has been. If there have been significant opportunities for students to engage in public-facing work, especially advocacy—the legislature is in session and available, students have had multiple travel opportunities to meet legislators and testify at hearings, etc.—then a private presentation and celebration might be fine. However, if the outside world has been relatively closed off due to logistics or other obstacles, then a chance to invite guests to a culminating event can add a public component to the course. This can help enrich the experience for students by making learning more transparent and discussable.

How should you address the fate of your students' bills?

As noted throughout this book, the context for legislative policymaking varies across states. Legislatures may not even be in session during class times, so that no action on a bill can be taken at all. On the other hand, bills can sometimes languish for extended periods in full-time legislatures due to a lack of urgency. Bills that are acted upon can meet many different fates, from quick committee deaths to the purgatory of continuation to successful passage.

Hopefully, you have worked throughout the course to prepare students for this variety of outcomes and have emphasized the journey over the destination. End-of-course activities and assignments should continue to focus on the overall experience rather than bill outcomes. Assignments and public presentations should emphasize skills development, lessons learned, the importance of civic engagement, and the often-long timeline of advocacy. If instructors choose to celebrate legislative successes, they should be wary of the dangers of making other students feel inadequate due to their lack of similar success. Individual reflection assignments might be a better avenue for exploring student concerns and feelings about bill success or failure.

How should you assess learning outcomes?

Learning outcomes will, of course, vary depending upon the various contexts discussed above, including the discipline in which the ENACT course has been situated. (Learning objectives are discussed in chapter 1, with some sample options included.) Some learning outcomes will have already been assessed in earlier assignments. For example, if one outcome is "demonstrating depth of knowledge in a policy area," then assignments like the legislative research report and one-pager may already be used to assess that outcome.

Still, end-of-term activities and assignments are likely to address at least some of the course's learning outcomes. Again, these outcomes should focus not on bill success, but on the skills and knowledge developed during the advocacy process. Outcomes might address the basic communication and collaboration skills that are part of most active learning. There are a variety of rubrics developed for presentation skills, knowledge articulation, and teamwork and collaboration skills that can be deployed here, or you can develop your own rubrics.

On the other hand, there are likely to be learning outcomes to address the more specific advocacy skills and knowledge of the legislative and advocacy process that the ENACT course aims to foster. You could assess these skills through a traditional examination, but such an exam seems to run counter to the spirit of the course, if not the goals; a traditional exam may seem ill-suited for the kinds of active learning and engagement activities of an ENACT experience. Instead, you may find that a public presentation or demonstration of advocacy as described in some of the activities suggested below may be better suited to this course. If you require some written artifacts from the course, you can also assign accompanying written reports or ask students to compile a portfolio for assessment (see below).

Assignments and Other Key Course Components

Present and Defend Event

The original Brandeis model for ENACT culminates in an activity known as "present and defend." The activity is designed to both incorporate community members (whether on campus or beyond) and encourage students to demonstrate their knowledge and engage in dialogue with others. If you conduct this exercise, you may invite legislators and staffers, members of advocacy coalitions and other community partners, and members of the campus community. You can also encourage students to invite friends and family members, in line with a more expanded notion of community and care (see below).

Typically, the activity is organized in a roundtable format with two or three timed conversations. Invited participants rotate among different tables to hear student presentations and ask questions about the bill. Students can develop more formal presentations, with an opening and closing statement in favor of their chosen bill, or may engage in more informal dialogue with participants at their tables. (See below.)

You can treat these conversations as formal, evaluated speaking assignments with goals, expectations, and grading rubrics or as more informal opportunities to demonstrate their learning. Whether the activity is graded or not, the event can be presented to students as a chance to demonstrate to both their audience and themselves just how far they've come in terms of advocacy skills and knowledge about their bills.

Community Celebration Event

The community celebration event, like the present and defend event, gives students the opportunity to present their advocacy work in a public setting. It differs from the present and defend activity in both tone and purpose, although many of the recommendations for this event that follow can also be incorporated into a more formal activity like present and defend. Students are not asked to prove their expertise through rigorous questioning about their bill. Instead, the community celebration event is an opportunity for students to present their advocacy work to the community and invite them to take action on the students' bills. Further, it provides students with the opportunity to talk with the community about what they have learned about democracy through engaging in advocacy work and what they see as possibilities for democracy in their communities. The celebration is meant to highlight students' accomplishments over the course of the semester, while also establishing a positive, fun, and supportive environment that may encourage others to see the work of advocacy and democracy as something they could do, and enjoy, as well.

The community celebration event is paired with the final presentation assignment (below). In the weeks leading up to the community celebration, the instructor invites the university community to attend the event. Students are encouraged to invite people from their communities to attend as well. At previous celebrations, students have brought their spouses or partners, children, friends, roommates, and neighbors. Students have invited coworkers, members of their places of worship, and people from other community organizations. Students are encouraged to invite people they care about and whom they would like to know more about their work.

The community celebration begins with some welcoming remarks and some unstructured time for socializing and sharing a meal. Beginning this way serves many purposes. First, it provides students with some time to settle in and relax their nerves before their presentations. Second, it allows for late arrivals to make a graceful entrance. The more community members who attend who are unfamiliar with the university campus, the more your scheduling should assume that people will be late. Third, it establishes the celebratory tone. While a catered lunch or dinner can make the event feel very special, even just cupcakes and coffee would be enough. When we share food together, we create community. Therefore, providing some food is an important element of the event.

After some time to eat, meet, and mingle, student presentations begin (see below). Each team presents their bill and invites audience members to take an action to support their bill. Students bring handouts for attendees to help them take action on their bill; sometimes that means sample social media posts, while in others it means sample scripts for calling their legislators. It is up to each team to decide what their ask will be, but each team is required to make at least one ask of the community.

After presenting their bill and advocacy work and making an ask of the audience, each student on the team reflects on their feelings about democracy and empowerment. They tell stories about their initial feelings of intimidation at the capitol, including feeling that they did not know enough or did not belong in the environment. They share stories about transformation, how they came to see their presence at the capitol as necessary, their voices as authoritative, their presence as powerful. Often, they describe how the experiences in the ENACT course have already empowered them to help people in their community. Students recount helping friends and relatives access legislators' constituent services to get problems solved for their loved ones or teaching friends how to find out who their legislator is and call on an issue they care about. In the course, students learn that they have what it takes to exercise power. At the community celebration they share their learning with the community and invite them into building power with them.

Final Presentation Assignment

Often, advocates will meet with community groups to educate them about important bills and ask them to take action. For the final assignment, students prepare a ten-minute presentation appropriate for a public audience. In this presentation, they are asked to:

- Explain the problem the bill is meant to solve.
- Educate the audience about the bill and how it addresses the problem.
- Explain the stakes by illustrating the negative consequences of inaction.
- Invite the audience to take a specific action to support the bill (for example, call their legislator, post to social media, etc.).

Students prepare slides for their presentation. They may also choose to create handouts for the audience to assist them in taking action on their bill. These handouts can include information about how to find out who their representative is, sample scripts for calling and leaving a message, sample social media posts with instructions for tagging legislators, and so on.

When offered as part of a community celebration, this assignment is meant to give students the opportunity to share their accomplishments with the public and invite others to take action on their issue. It is also meant to provide students with the opportunity to reflect on the possibility of democracy in their communities. After the public presentation, each student answers the following questions:

- What did you learn about democracy by taking part in this class?
- What opportunities are there for you and your communities to be engaged in democracy going forward?

Again, ending the presentations with these questions allows students the opportunity to reflect on the ethical and civic significance of their learning over the course while identifying possibilities for extending their participation. They also provide a starting point for further conversations with community members in attendance about possible next steps for staying involved. In this way, the final presentation assignment can give students the opportunity to connect their learning in the class to the people and communities they care about.

Lessons-Learned Presentation

Rather than focus on advocacy for their chosen issue or connecting their learning to the broader community, students can alternatively emphasize the advocacy skills and knowledge they have developed during the term. A "lessons learned" assignment typically involves a poster or presentation session that offers direct advice for advocates. The audience for these presentations can vary depending on logistics and instructor preference, but can include:

- Community partners who are participants in advocacy coalitions
- Future students of an ENACT course
- A broader audience of students who might be interested in advocacy or have opportunities to engage in advocacy in the future
- Legislators and staffers who might be interested in hearing insights about advocacy from those new to the process

ENACT students can try to share not just advice but also arguments for why advocacy and civic engagement are important. Personal reflections, similar to the ones described in the final presentation assignment above, can also be included. If desired, the presentation can be accompanied or followed by a written report that summarizes the presentation's findings.

Final Legislative Report Assignment

Students can be asked to update their legislative research report assignment (see chapter 3) from earlier in the term with new knowledge about the bill and policy issue, as well as feedback from peers, legislative meetings, faculty, and other stakeholders. Students could be asked to project and strategize about future advocacy and outcomes for the bill.

Reflection Assignments

As the final presentation assignment above shows, it is possible to include reflection as part of the group project experience in different types of culminating assignments. You can also consider including opportunities for private reflection. Carefully tailored writing assignments can help students identify what they may have learned about themselves, as well as about their values, concerns, passions, and interests. Meaningful opportunities for reflection can also ask students to envision a future that involves civic engagement, whether through employment in or around government or through civic participation outside of employment. Reflection prompts may offer broad questions about what students learned and how they feel about civic engagement; more specific prompts may ask them to imagine a future life as a legislator, staffer, or advocate.

Advocacy Portfolio

Another effective way for students to demonstrate learning across the ENACT course is to assemble portfolios of the work completed throughout the course, whether as individuals or as a group. Ideally, you would ask students to collect work throughout the term, including legislative research reports, one-pagers, and other advocacy materials. These can be combined with culminating thoughts and reflections, as well as thoughts about next steps, to provide a chance for both students and instructors to assess learning outcomes and the experience as a whole.

Additional Resources

While some aspects of the culminating projects described above involve looking back over the term, these assignments and activities also ask students to think about their lives going forward. You and your students can access additional resources to help with life after ENACT, including the following.

Campus Career Center

Whatever its title, probably every university or college has a career center of some sort. The staff there are often willing partners for collaborations that focus on job and career paths and might be able to offer a variety of resources. A center with strong connections in state government can help an instructor connect with employers, develop internship opportunities, and offer job and career counseling. Depending on the instructor's time and available space within the course, you could bring in a career counselor for a résumé workshop or to offer advice for work in state government. On some campuses, it may even be possible to organize a job fair with the theme of state government employment.

In terms of job and career paths, legislatures have varying degrees of professionalization that offer opportunities for employment. Most states offer staff jobs but can vary on how these are chosen. Beyond the legislature, any state government presents job opportunities and chances for careers with meaning and impact that are often overlooked in favor of private sector opportunities; ENACT courses present a chance to highlight these options for students, who may never have considered a career in public service.

Advising Resources

Students interested in a life in state government and advocacy might want more information about next steps *on* campus. Are there other relevant classes within the same or other major programs? Are there internships offered? How does an interest in advocacy affect their choice of major or classes within a major? One possible class activity could involve developing an advising plan, either for specific individuals or as part of the ENACT experience in general. Depending on the resources available on your campus, you might connect with advisors or advising functions to ensure that students' advocacy journey can be further developed in their future academic work.

Community Partners

In many cases, an ENACT course has just brought together a small community of legislators, staffers, and advocates to help guide students through the advocacy process. Either during that process or, as part of culminating experiences, it can be helpful for any or all of these partners to speak with students about jobs and careers. You can, and probably should, incorporate this into the regular business of contact points with any outside speaker or resource; as part of their interaction with the course, be sure to find time to ask them questions like "How did you get into this work? How can others?" Alternatively, you can organize a more formal panel of experts to illustrate varied job and career paths.

Networks developed before and during class can also be reviewed for paths to civic engagement more broadly. Certainly, advocacy coalitions offer models for jobs, as they often include paid advocates and nonprofit workers. But they also model participation in meaningful advocacy by volunteer participants, professional allies, and others. The ENACT experience offers an opportunity to encourage students to consider ways to remain engaged in advocacy no matter what their job might be in the future.

Social/Alumni Networks

If you decide to adapt ENACT at your institution—and fall in love with the model as we have!—you may end up offering it regularly as part of your course catalog. As a result, you will develop cohorts of ENACT course alumni. Such alumni, whether or not they continue in advocacy work, can become resources for future classes, both while they are on campus and then beyond. You can ask students from last year's class to offer "lessons learned" advice to this year's cohort, or you can bring in an alum to reflect on how their ENACT experience has led them to pursue citizen advocacy work in their own community. If you already have existing methods for staying connected with alumni, at the departmental or institutional level, you can use these to also remain connected with ENACT course veterans.

Department Internship Programs

Some individual academic departments, programs, and divisions have internship programs targeted at specific careers. The ENACT class can be a feeder to such programs in state government. When feasible, an ENACT instructor can also help shape those opportunities by ensuring that there are significant advocacy opportunities as part of internships. The networks you develop and coordinate might helpfully offer additional options for existing internship programs. Whether they are already developed or you are developing them, you can incorporate these future opportunities into the class by scheduling visits from internship coordinators and/or current and former interns.

Campus Volunteer/Service Programs

Most institutions feature an office, often in the college's student life functions, that helps promote service opportunities. At their worst these offices engage in hour-tracking exercises; still, most staff and students are much more interested in generating meaningful experiences that can help shape student character and offer welcome benefits to community partners. It can be worth connecting with such offices to see whether there are ways to catalog existing advocacy opportunities and possibly add more through community partners and other contacts, so that students can pursue more opportunities to advance their advocacy journeys—as well as provide helpful expertise that they've developed to partners who can use it.

Again, while you can bring in resources and speakers specifically to address career paths, you should consider incorporating such conversations throughout the course. Speakers and resources do not just offer advice for advocacy and getting the job done in the ENACT class, but also offer models for jobs, careers, and lives. If you make the value of advocacy and civic engagement part of the conversation from the beginning, students are much more likely to take civic engagement seriously both during and after the ENACT experience.

Conclusion

Data and experience suggest ENACT can be a powerful and transformative experience for students, with long-lasting effects. The scaffolding provided by a successful send-off can help them place this experience in context. Ideally, students will feel empowered to build a path going forward that recognizes the importance of advocacy and civic engagement, whether or not they do it for a living.

I feel I gained a more nuanced understanding of how long it truly takes to get a bill to pass—even on the state level—from this course. As a healthcare nonprofit employee, we are often advocating for bills that would better the health of people in our state or increase better health outcomes. The course definitely gave me a more realistic view of how advocacy work takes place and how many cycles we can be discussing the same bill with our donors and supporters.

—from a survey of Brandeis alumni who participated in ENACT course

As with everything ENACT, you should consider your own goals and preferences, comfort level, and institutional context before selecting culminating experiences. Still, whatever you choose to incorporate into your ENACT course, we encourage you to engage in these activities in a spirit of celebration. Students have had a special experience in their advocacy work and marking it clearly is important.

Consider any culminating moment in class as an opportunity to celebrate your students. Food is highly recommended, especially if you are welcoming in community partners and friends from outside the class. In general, such end-of-term celebrations are unfortunately rare; students often leave an academic experience with a (punishing?) final assessment, drifting off into a break one by one as they are released from a crowded classroom. Instead, a culminating celebration offers a chance to put a nice bow on the class. It can leave everyone, including the instructor, with a sense of accomplishment and camaraderie with hopefully lasting effects on community building for your class, in your department or program, and on your campus more broadly.

Sample Assignment Guidelines for Present and Defend Activity

Assignment. Each team will have *20 minutes* to convince the audience to support its legislation. The audience will role-play as policymaker staff and interested citizens.

There are multiple possible approaches to the oral presentation. You might use your elevator speech, information from your legislative research report or one-pager, parts of your video assignment, or something else.

In general, your presentation should include the following components:

- Overview and bill description
- Statement of the problem and how the bill addresses (or does *not* address) the problem
- Stakeholders and affected parties
- Next steps: What you would focus on if you continued work on the bill
- Please leave plenty of time for questions from the audience

Your presentation will be graded on the following criteria:

- Level of preparedness
- Evidence of maturation in understanding the legislative process
- Level of understanding of the issue
- Ability to handle questions and comments
- Quality of materials presented
- Quality of communication skills
- Teamwork/collaborative effort

Sample Assignment Guidelines for Final Presentation/Community Celebration

Assignment. One of the most important skills successful advocates must develop is the ability to speak publicly about their issue. Advocates must be able to effectively communicate information about their bill and the legislative process while also getting people excited about their issue. Publicly presenting your work is crucial to bringing people in and building your base of power.

For the final assignment of the class, students will present their work to the class and any guests who attend on the final day. Each presentation will have two parts:

Part I: The Public Presentation (10 minutes)

Students will give a public presentation of their bill to the audience. The goal of the public presentation is to get audience members to understand

and support your bill. You'll need to inform the audience about your bill and explain why it's important and what they can do to take action to support it.

Groups should make sure to present in an engaging way. Remember, every conversation is an opportunity to build power! Don't forget to end with a call to action!

Part II: Reflection (2–3 minutes per person)

Each member of the group will share a brief reflection on what they learned about our democracy by participating in the class. Here are some questions for you to consider as you prepare for your reflection:

- What did you believe about our legislature and politicians before this class? Has what you learned changed your views?
- What did you believe about your own power as a citizen before this class? Has what you learned changed your views?
- How would you assess the health of our democracy in our state? Is it possible for the people to participate? What constraints make it difficult? What enables participation?
- What could we do to make our democracy better for the people and communities we love in our state?
- In what ways do you plan to use your power in the future?

Note: Student presentations should not be just a list of answers to these questions. These questions are just meant to get you started thinking about your experience. You should write a reflection that exhibits your own thinking and your own style.

Students will turn in presentation materials for grading. Students' grades will be based on both the quality of the materials and the quality of the final presentation in class.

Sample Assignment Guidelines for Lessons-Learned Presentation

Assignment. You've already completed some reflections based on your experiences in this course. You'll now formalize some of these reflections, as well as any other conclusions from your work in the course, into a presentation that collects the "lessons learned" by your group. You'll share this presentation with a varied audience—legislators and "friends of the class," as well as fellow students in the department, who will be invited to a public presentation session.

Format. Your presentation should include the following elements/slides:

- *Title Slide*: Include a descriptive title, authors, and affiliation
- *Bill Background*: Number and title of the bill you worked on
  - Include a short description, ideally in bullet points
  - Identify key arguments you made for the bill (these can be pulled from your factsheet/storybook and/or legislative research report)
- *Lessons Learned*: At least three bullet points
  - Based on your experiences as a student in this class, what do you think were the key things you learned about policy advocacy? (Examples would help.)
- *Future Advice for Advocacy*: At least two bullet points
  - Based on what you learned from speakers and your own experiences, what advice do you have for future ENACT students and/or policy advocates in general? (Again, use examples.)
- *Future Advice for ENACT courses*: At least two bullet points
  - What could the instructor in this course (or, really, *any* policy advocacy course) do differently in the future to improve student learning and experience?

NOTE

1. Mary Ryan, "The Pedagogical Balancing Act: Teaching Reflection in Higher Education," *Teaching in Higher Education* 18, no. 2 (2013): 144–55.

Conclusion

THIS BOOK began by acknowledging the consensus about a crisis in civic education, with troubling consequences for our democracy. Indeed, the problems our polity faces are numerous and challenging: climate change, persistent inequality, crippling political polarization, and massive institutions (both public and private) that often do not seem up to meeting these challenges.

A college course might seem like an odd choice for a response. Certainly, we do not claim that ENACT by itself solves all or even one of these problems. One course cannot change the world.

And yet! The authors of this volume all believe that we can and should take action to combat both these problems and the seeming increase in cynicism about the ability to solve them. We strongly feel that as educators, with responsibility for shaping the next generation of transformational leaders, we should do *something*. The fact that you are reading this book means that you probably agree.

We do not want to sound grandiose. But our experiences as ENACT instructors tell us that the ENACT advocacy course offers an important intervention in this civic crisis, with positive consequences for students and instructors. In the rest of this brief conclusion, we want to present some initial evidence about ENACT's effects in more detail, as well as offer some reflections and suggestions about what ENACT might do for you and your students. If, after getting through this entire volume, you are still on the fence about whether or not to take on ENACT, we hope this final word will give you the extra push you need.

The Evidence

There is mounting evidence that ENACT is an effective model for countering some of the problems described in the civic "crisis" literature earlier in this book. Certainly, such positive effects are supported by our experiences as ENACT faculty—widely shared, we should note, among other instructors in the ENACT network—as well as data gathered by ENACT's home at Brandeis University and other ENACT researchers.

Promising data was already produced in a study by four ENACT faculty—most of whom are authors of this book—already briefly cited in the Introduction.[1] Drawing on a broad literature on measures of civic engagement, the authors conducted a survey asking students questions about their own levels of political engagement, action, and efficacy, as well as political expression and knowledge. We should note that ENACT students generally scored higher on pretest estimates; ENACT courses, unsurprisingly, are likely to draw students who already show some minimal interest in politics. Still, ENACT students showed measurably greater increases on some measures than students in control classes that offered more "traditional" models of political science instruction. As the authors of that article noted:

> Students in all courses reported increases in political knowledge, with no significant differences between the course types. This should not be surprising, since all political science courses regardless of pedagogical approach aim to increase political knowledge and understanding. While both types of courses are associated with increases in students' perceptions of political knowledge, the ENACT focus on experiential learning seems to do a significantly better job at boosting perceptions of civic engagement, political efficacy, and civic action.[2]

The varying results on different measures, in our view, makes the ENACT results even more robust. The lack of variation on knowledge suggests that if you want to teach students about politics, they can learn that in a traditional course setting. But if you want them to *engage* in politics—and if you want to help address the civic crisis that seems pressing—the ENACT model may provide an effective way to start.

This study covered an admittedly small number of cases. But subsequent research from the network, including a large multicenter study that is currently ongoing, also shows similar results. For this study, ENACT's leadership team joined with a group of faculty fellows to develop a survey instrument based on national evaluation tools. The resulting ENACT National Survey has been administered to over 240 students from over twenty different participating institutions since January 2022. ENACT leaders have published the results in a number of reports, including a 2024 update.[3] Key findings from the 2024 report include the following:

- Students who participate in ENACT courses report high levels of political efficacy, with 89% agreeing that they "know enough to participate in politics" and 79% saying that they are "better informed about politics and government than most people." Survey researchers were able to separate out participants in courses with core "direct lobbying" experiences, and these respondents reported even higher levels of agreement with the statement "I can influence politics or policy in my community/state," 81% to 76%.
- ENACT students report much higher rates of voting than typical turnout percentages, particularly when compared to the demographic of traditional college-aged students who currently make up the bulk of ENACT participants. These results were particularly (and probably not surprisingly) robust on the state and local level, with over 50% reporting participation in their last state election and 44% in their last local election, considerably higher than most reported totals for such elections nationally.

ENACT researchers have also conducted qualitative studies that suggest even more robust effects. A pilot survey of 51 Brandeis alumni (out of 247) who had taken the original ENACT course was conducted in 2021 and published in 2022.[4] Respondents to this survey reported dramatically higher rates of specific civic engagement activity than national samples. Aside from similarly high voter turnout rates, 60% of respondents reported contacting an elected official in the previous twelve months, as compared to 19% nationally (as reported by the Public Religion Research Institute). A similarly large cohort reported volunteering with a group or cause (49% ENACT to 19% nationally) or donating money to a campaign or cause (80% to 19%).

Certainly there may be some self-selection in these results, as the type of students who gravitate to ENACT courses may be the ones who would report these activities anyway. And much more work still needs to be done by ENACT researchers to compare and calibrate results against national measures. Still, the evidence points toward significant impact on student outcomes. The pilot results from Brandeis alumni, both on the survey and on subsequent interviews conducted with a handful of participants, include a number of reports of students pursuing social justice work or legal careers because of their ENACT experience. Indeed, over 70% of respondents agreed that the ENACT course had impacted their professional journey.

All of these study results confirm the anecdotal experiences of ENACT faculty. Like the example of the baseball players provided at the very beginning of this volume, we have watched students from our ENACT courses go on to careers in state politics, from staff positions to government affairs and nonprofit advocacy to, in at least one case, an elected state official. As some of our authors argued in another publication, "Demanding educational experiences such as [ENACT] are the very settings in which the qualities of political leadership are forged."[5] More importantly, wherever our students end up, many seem to take this experience of active engagement and the ability to effectively participate in the political process with them, making them better citizens.

> *I realized that the government isn't as "far away" and "unapproachable" as I thought, especially every time I got to the statehouse and actually talked to and met people in the legislative offices.*
>
> —response from ENACT survey, Brandeis University

Transforming Political Science Education

In 2024, a task force from the American Political Science Association released its report on "Rethinking Political Science Education." According to the report, the task force had been convened as a response to both recent events, such as the Covid-19 pandemic and the January 6 uprising, and long-term trends in higher education and the world. Besides these challenges, the report notes, "There is also the realization, reinforced by current events, that there needs to be great emphasis on promoting the development of democratic citizenship."[6] Our students will need the skills and values that a robust civic education can provide in order to take their place as the next generation of transformative leaders.

The task force's report includes a number of recommendations for changes to political science education, particularly focused on offering a series of global learning objectives for the discipline organized into three categories of content, skills, and values. We believe that ENACT, as a pedagogical model, offers a way of addressing all three of these categories. Some particularly salient objectives include the following:

- *Content Learning Objective 4: Explain and evaluate the effectiveness and ethics of different strategies of civic engagement at the local, regional, national, and global levels.* ENACT courses provide opportunities for students to learn, practice, and implement effective civic engagement strategies at the state level. In many versions of ENACT, their practice also immerses them in thinking about advocacy and engagement at multiple levels of government, as well as considering ethical obligations and strategic objectives while completing their advocacy projects.
- *Skills Learning Objective 2: Engage as citizens through problem solving, collective action, and collaborative decision-making at all levels from local to global.* Again, ENACT is very much a skills-based course, with students working collaboratively to address community issues through state legislative advocacy. Those ENACT experiences that connect students to existing advocacy coalitions offer particularly robust opportunities to consider and practice collective action skills.
- *Values Learning Objective 1: Demonstrate an understanding of civic dispositions conducive to democratic involvement.* Through both practice and reflection, ENACT students are asked to develop these civic dispositions and reflect on the importance and purpose of political engagement.

Most versions of an ENACT course are very likely to address some additional objectives defined by the task force. For example, the legislative research report can help students practice the key skill of citing evidence, and almost all the assignments outlined in this volume offer opportunities for students to work on their communication skills.

Of course, not every ENACT instructor will come from the discipline of political science, nor will they see any kind of obligation to address any of the task force's concerns. Still, the concerns the task force is raising and trying to address are much broader than the needs of any educational discipline. Again, the broader concerns about civic engagement and democracy raised at the beginning of this book should be of concern to all educators and citizens. While no single college course can be a magic bullet to restore democratic values, we believe that ENACT represents exactly the kind of pedagogical intervention needed at this time.

Enacting ENACT

And so: we encourage you to teach ENACT on your own campus. We have broken down the ENACT experience into its component parts so as to make it easier to digest and implement. Still, we recognize that even this modular approach offers a very large menu of options that can seem like a daunting to-do list. We again will remind you that ENACT is flexible, modular, and adaptable to many different campus and political circumstances.

As a final incentive to adopt ENACT, you might consider your own circumstances and environment. What are your personal and career goals and passions? And how might ENACT meet those goals and feed those passions? For example, you might consider the following questions:

- Have you been looking for a new course offering? Perhaps you are expanding the options for your political science major or looking to add interdisciplinary options to your program. ENACT might enhance your department's offerings or meet student demands, especially in challenging resource environments where administrators are paying careful attention to course enrollments and variety.
- Are there on-campus programs, such as honors or first-year seminars, that are looking for new approaches and ideas for engaging course material? ENACT might be easier to implement in such programs, which often allow for innovative and diverse course proposals without strict disciplinary needs and guidelines.
- Are you looking for active learning interventions or ways to make your course material come alive in connection with problem-solving and real-world applications? ENACT might meet these needs in a particularly robust and innovative way, addressing the civic crisis while also drawing more students to your classes.
- Are you looking for ways to more actively engage students in making an impact in the world? Again, ENACT offers measurable impacts on student engagement and feelings of efficacy. You can provide opportunities to show students they *can* make a difference in the world, as well as *how* they can do it.

On this last point, we should note that faculty are not immune to the cynicism and malaise that sometimes seem to infect our politics. Frustration with partisan gridlock, cynicism about self-serving officials, and "doom scrolling" to despair may sometimes feel like the only sane way to respond to our current political circumstances. Alternatively, it might seem easier to retreat into ivory tower isolation and try to insulate both you and your students from the rest of the world through abstract concepts and teaching.

Our experience is that getting students out into the world in the way that ENACT does brings with it something vital that is often lost in the day-to-day grind of teaching: *hope*. Our participation in ENACT has made us more hopeful—for change, for the ability of our polity to solve our greatest challenges, for our students, and for the future. ENACT still requires the mundane details of education, with paperwork to be done and grades to file. Still, such seeming drudgery always seems easier for us to complete after leaving a final present and defend event or community celebration or hearing or reading student reflections about their accomplishments and hopes for the future.

We do not think you should avoid the facts of our current politics in your classes; sometimes our leaders *are* self-serving, and certain features of our political system *do* suffer from dysfunction. But you can decide how to engage students in addressing these problems in ways that do not encourage despair. The authors of this book have all found engaging in ENACT to be productive and fruitful. We see how good it is for students to understand—*really* understand—how politics works, as well as how there is a place for them in the process. You don't have to be a Pollyanna about political change. But again, you can show students that there is still something to be done, and how to do it.

Once more we will remind you that you do *not* have to do everything all at once. The core experience of ENACT involves bringing students to the state legislature and immersing them in that environment, and we still hope you can find a way to make that happen for students on your campus. Students not only learn about representation and observe the rituals of power politics, but an in-person visit also helps them viscerally feel the "buzz" of the building: legislators rushing to hearings, overworked staffers answering multiple phones, uniformed pages running fresh copies of bills to the floor. It's exciting! But when a legislator takes time to sit down to meet with them and answer their questions even if they are not supporting the bill, students recognize their own power to participate. They may not get their bill over the finish line, but they can learn to see the next opportunity for change. And they can greet that opportunity with hope and energy.

And as much as visiting the capitol is important, ENACT students can find that hope and energy in multiple ways. Maybe you do not have the resources or time—yet!—to make trips to the legislature happen. You can still host speakers, engage in virtual meetings, write letters to the editor, or develop mock one-pagers. You can model different parts of the experience and incorporate them into other classes, enhancing the material and helping students make connections. You can make policy and politics come alive, in whatever way is feasible to you on your campus.

ENACT has been challenging, but also immensely rewarding. We encourage you to use the resources in this book. Make a plan, for you and your students. ENACT change. You—and your students—will be glad that you did.

> *My experience in the class gave me the confidence to become more involved in the political process. I learned that I do have some power to make a difference.*
>
> —response from ENACT alumni survey, Brandeis University

NOTES

1. Robert W. Glover et al., "Advocating for Engagement: Do Experiential Learning Courses Boost Civic Engagement?" *Journal of Political Science Education* 17, Supp. 1 (2021): 599–615.

2. Glover et al., "Advocating for Engagement," 610.

3. Kaitie Chakoian, Charlotte Powley, and Melissa Stimell, *Transformations Through Civic Engagement: A National Evaluation of the Impact of the ENACT Course on Student Attitudes, Knowledge, and Behavior*, vol. 2 (Waltham, MA: Brandeis University, 2024).

4. Kaitie Chakoian, Charlotte Powley, and Melissa Stimell, *Transforming the Civic Engagement of Future Generations: A Pilot Evaluation of the Impact of the ENACT Course on Alumni Civic Engagement and Career Trajectories* (Waltham, MA: Brandeis University, 2022).

5. Robert W. Glover, Kathleen Cole, and Katharine Owens, "ENACT-ing Leadership at the State Level: A National Educational Network for Engaged Citizenship in State Legislatures," *Maine Policy Review* 27, No. 1 (2018): 22–26.

6. APSA Presidential Task Force on Rethinking Political Science Education, *Rethinking Political Science Education* (Washington, DC: American Political Science Association, 2024), 10.

Acknowledgments

Kathleen Cole would like to thank everyone who has made it possible to teach this course in Minnesota: all the legislators, legislative assistants, legislative librarians, newspaper editors, lobbyists, organizers, and staff in the Governor's Office who have so generously given their time and expertise to the course. She would also like to thank her students for doing the hard work to make Minnesota better for the people and communities they love.

Rob Glover would like to thank his students. Without fail, they bring their energy and civic enthusiasm to each iteration of his ENACT course, ensuring that each semester is uniquely rewarding. They enrich the experience for him, their classmates, and all of the legislators, staffers, and policy advocates with whom they interact.

Richard Meagher would like to thank the legislators, staffers, and policy advocates and experts who have almost universally answered the call to help guide students through their ENACT experiences. He would also like to thank his wife and two daughters for the support through various disappearances for ENACT-related work.

Katharine Owens would like to thank her family for constant support and understanding, her friends for reminding her to relax, and her students for making every semester more interesting than the last.

The authors would like to collectively thank Sue Berger Ramin, Ashley Burns, and the rest of the staff at Brandeis University Press for editing and guidance. We would also like to thank all of our ENACT fellows, past and present. By generously sharing their time and work, they have contributed greatly to our understanding of ENACT and have been considerate and collaborative thought partners as we have navigated implementing this model over the years. We would particularly like to thank Michelle Inderbitzen for her contributions to planning this volume.

Finally, the authors would like to thank the ENACT leadership at Brandeis University, particularly: Daniel Terris, who first welcomed us all to Brandeis, and to ENACT; Charlotte Powley and Kaitie Chakoian, who generously shared their research and support for this project; David J. Weinstein, for his years of cheerful and capable support, camaraderie, and leadership; and, finally, Melissa Stimell, whose innovative teaching inspired a national network, and who has since guided and sustained us through the years with advice, encouragement, and the occasional ice cream cone.

Bibliography

Abernathy, Penelope Muse. *News Deserts and Ghost Newspapers: Will Local News Survive?* Chapel Hill, NC: University of North Carolina Press, 2020.

Americans' Dismal Views of the Nation's Politics. Washington, DC: Pew Research Center, 2023.

APSA Presidential Task Force on Rethinking Political Science Education. *Rethinking Political Science Education.* Washington, DC: American Political Science Association, 2024.

APSA Task Force on Civic Education in the 21st Century. "Expanded Articulation Statement: A Call for Reactions and Contributions." *PS: Political Science & Politics* 31, no. 1 (March 1998): 363–38.

Baskin-Sommers, Arielle, Cortney Simmons, May Conley, and B. J. Casey. "Adolescent Civic Engagement: Lessons from Black Lives Matter." *Proceedings of the National Academy of Sciences* 118, no. 41 (December 2021). www.pnas.org/content/118/41/e2109860118.

Bell, Lauren C., Allison Rank, and Carah Ong Whaley, eds. *Civic Pedagogies: Teaching Civic Engagement in an Era of Divisive Politics.* New York: Palgrave Macmillan, 2024.

Bennion, Elizabeth A., and Xander E. Laughlin. "Best Practices in Civic Education: Lessons from the *Journal of Political Science Education.*" *Journal of Political Science Education* 14, no. 3 (January 2018): 287–330.

Bhojwani, Sayu. *People Like Us: The New Wave of Candidates Knocking at Democracy's Door.* New York: The New Press, 2018.

Carroll, Morgan. *Take Back Your Government: A Citizen's Guide to Grassroots Change.* Chicago: Fulcrum, 2012.

Chakoian, Kaitie, Charlotte Powley, and Melissa Stimell. *Transformations Through Civic Engagement: A National Evaluation of the Impact of the ENACT Course on Student Attitudes, Knowledge, and Behavior*, Volume 2. Waltham, MA: Brandeis University, 2024.

Chakoian, Kaitie, Charlotte Powley, and Melissa Stimell. *Transforming the Civic Engagement of Future Generations: A Pilot Evaluation of the Impact of the ENACT Course on Alumni Civic Engagement and Career Trajectories.* Waltham, MA: Brandeis University Press, 2022.

DePalo, Kathryn A. *The Failure of Term Limits in Florida.* Gainesville, FL: University Press of Florida, 2015.

Derek Bok Center for Teaching and Learning, Harvard University. "ABLConnect." Accessed July 1, 2024. https://ablconnect.harvard.edu.

Elazar, Daniel J. *American Federalism: A View from the States.* New York: Thomas Y. Crowell, 1966.

Emeran, Christine. "The March for Our Lives Movement in the United States: Generational Change and the Personalization of Protest." In *When Students Protest: Secondary and High Schools*, edited by Judith Bessant, Analicia Mejia Mesinas, and Sarah Pickard, 145–60. Lanham, MD: Rowman & Littlefield, 2021.

ENACT. "ENACT: The Educational Network for Active Civic Transformation." Accessed July 1, 2024. www.brandeis.edu/enact.

ENACT. "Program Components." Accessed July 1, 2024. www.brandeis.edu/enact/program-components.html.

ENACT. "Public Resources." Accessed July 1, 2024. www.enactnetwork.org/resources/view/public.

Ferguson, Dana. "'Opportunity to Make History': Communities of Color Look to Lawmakers to Close Gaps." *MPRNews*, February 13, 2023. www.mprnews.org/story/2023/02/13/opportunity-to-make-history-communities-of-color-look-to-lawmakers-to-close-gaps.

Forman-Katz, Naomi, Elisa Shearer, and Katerina Eva Matsa. "Nonprofit News Outlets Are Playing a Growing Role In Statehouse Coverage." Washington, DC: Pew Research Center, 2022. www.pewresearch.org/short-reads/2022/04/29/nonprofit-news-outlets-are-playing-a-growing-role-in-statehouse-coverage.

Fried, Amy, and Douglas B. Harris. *At War with Government: How Conservatives Weaponized Distrust from Goldwater to Trump*. New York: Columbia University Press, 2021.

Glover, Robert W., Kathleen Cole, and Katharine Owens. "ENACT-ing Leadership at the State Level: A National Educational Network for Engaged Citizenship in State Legislatures." *Maine Policy Review* 27, No. 1 (2018): 22–26.

Glover, Robert W., Daniel C. Lewis, Richard Meagher, and Katherine A. Owens. "Advocating for Engagement: Do Experiential Learning Courses Boost Civic Engagement?" *Journal of Political Science Education* 17, Supp. 1 (2021): 599–615.

Gold Standard PBL: Essential Project Design Elements. Novato, CA: Buck Institute for Education, 2015.

Hay, Colin. *Why We Hate Politics*. Cambridge, UK: Polity Press, 2007.

Hibbing, John R., and Elizabeth Theiss-Morse. *Stealth Democracy: Americans' Beliefs About How Government Should Work*. Cambridge, UK: Cambridge University Press, 2002.

Jensen, Barbara. *Reading Classes: On Culture and Classism in America*. Ithaca, NY: ILR Press, 2012.

Jerit, Jennifer, and Yangzi Zhao. "Political Misinformation." *Annual Review of Political Science* 23, no. 1 (May 2020): 77–94.

National Conference of State Legislatures. "The Term-Limited States." Last modified August 3, 2023. www.ncsl.org/about-state-legislatures/the-term-limited-states.

National Conference of State Legislatures. "2024 State Legislative Session Calendar." Last modified July 8, 2024. www.ncsl.org/about-state-legislatures/2024-state-legislative-session-calendar/.

O'Brien, Karen, Elin Selboe, and Bronwyn M. Hayward. "Exploring Youth Activism on Climate Change: Dutiful, Disruptive, and Dangerous Dissent." *Ecology and Society* 23, no. 3 (2018): 42. https://doi.org/10.5751/ES-10287-230342.

PBLWorks. "Projects and Resources." Accessed July 1, 2024. www.pblworks.org/resources-overview.

Redman, Eric. *The Dance of Legislation: An Insider's Account of the Workings of the United States Senate*. Seattle: University of Washington Press, 2011.

Reingold, Beth. "Gender, Race/Ethnicity, and Representation in State Legislatures." *PS: Political Science & Politics* 52, no. 3 (2019): 426–29.

Resource Generation. "Class Distinctions & Income Brackets." Accessed July 1, 2024. https://resourcegeneration.org/breakdown-of-class-characteristics-income-brackets.

Robey, Janet. "What Is Crossover Day?" Concerned Women of America Legislative Action Committee. Last modified January 30, 2021. https://concernedwomen.org/what-is-crossover-day.

Rosenthal, Alan. *Engines of Democracy: Politics and Policymaking in State Legislatures*. Washington, DC: CQ Press, 2009.

Ryan, Mary. "The Pedagogical Balancing Act: Teaching Reflection in Higher Education." *Teaching in Higher Education* 18, no. 2 (2013): 144–55.

Schaar, Susan Clarke. *Your Guide to the Virginia General Assembly*. Richmond, VA: Virginia Senate Clerk's Office, n.d.

State Legislators: Who They Are and How to Work with Them. Washington, DC: National Conference of State Legislators, 2018.

Strachan, J. Cherie. "Student and Civic Engagement: Cultivating the Skills, Efficacy and Identities That Increase Student Involvement in Learning and in Public Life." In *Handbook on Teaching and Learning in Political Science and International Relations*, edited by John Ishiyama, William J. Miller, and Simon Eszter, 60–73. Northampton, MA: Edward Elgar, 2015.

Stroozas, Sam. "'Shaking Things Up': Minnesota's LGBTQ Lawmakers See New Strength at Capitol." *MPRNews*, January 17, 2023. www.mprnews.org/story/2023/01/17/were-shaking-things-up-minnesotas-lgbtq-lawmakers-see-new-strength-at-capitol.

The 2023–2024 Guide to the Nevada Legislature. Carson City, NV: Research Division, Nevada Legislative Counsel Bureau, 2023.

Thompson, Neil B. *Minnesota's State Capitol: The Art and Politics of a Public Building*. St. Paul: Minnesota Historical Society Press, 1974.

"Tool: Laser Talk." *The Leading Teacher*. Fall 2012. https://learningforward.org/wp-content/uploads/2012/08/tools-laser-talks.pdf.

Washington State Legislature. "Glossary of Legislative Terms." Accessed July 1, 2024. https://app.leg.wa.gov/billinfo/glossary.aspx#B.

Contributors

KATHLEEN COLE is a professor of political science and chair of the Social Science Department at Metropolitan State University in Minneapolis–St. Paul, Minnesota. As an organizer, she focuses on the abolition of police and prisons and the establishment of care infrastructure. Her research has been published in *Politics, Groups, and Identities* and *Political Science Education.*

ROBERT W. GLOVER is an associate professor of political science and honors at the University of Maine in Orono. He is co-director of the Maine Chapter of the Scholars Strategy Network. His recent research projects have examined drug policy attitude formation and citizen involvement in election administration. He is co-editor of a multivolume series on honors education from Rowman and Littlefield and of *Teaching Politics Beyond the Book.*

RICHARD J. MEAGHER is a professor of political science at Randolph-Macon College in Ashland, Virginia. He is a faculty fellow for both ENACT and the Network for Vocational Undergraduate Education (NetVUE) and the author of *Local Politics Matters.*

KATHARINE A. OWENS is a professor of politics, economics, and international studies and director of the Rell Center for Public Service at the University of Hartford in Connecticut. She is both a National Geographic Explorer and a Fulbright-Nehru Scholar, and her research has been published in *Frontiers in Environmental Science* and *Sustainability.*

MELISSA STIMELL is the director of ENACT: The Abraham Feinberg Educational Network for Active Civic Transformation. She is a professor of the Practice in the Legal Studies Program and chair of the Program in Social Justice and Social Policy at Brandeis University. She has been a public interest attorney for over thirty years, focusing on the representation of vulnerable populations in such areas as criminal law, discrimination of individuals with disabilities, and child welfare.

Index

ABLConnect, 24
academic internship, 19–20
active learning, 63
activism, 22
activity-based learning, 24
adaptability, 102–3, 110
advising resources, 156
advocacy flier, 72–74, 85–91
advocacy organizations, 75, 128, 136
advocacy portfolio, 155
advocacy position, 70
advocacy video, 145
advocates/citizen advocates: advocacy coalitions and, 157; characteristics of, 59, 67; community groups and, 153; defined, 59; effectiveness of, 2; for ENACT course, 22; expertise of, 59, 66, 70; harm from, 64; higher education, 68; honesty of, 67; legislative relationships with, 41; legitimacy of, 64; lessons learned assignment for, 154; one-pager of, 72–73; passion of, 59; policy, 46–47; political organizers and, 43; public speaking by, 160; social media and, 132–33; students as, 99 (*see also* students)
Alaska, 60
alumni, 49, 61, 157, 165–66
American Association of University Professors (AAUP), 62
American East Coast, 142
American Genius, 118–19
American Medical Association, 28
American Political Science Association, 166
Amesbury, Massachusetts, 143
animal portraits, 134–35
Anishinaabe people, 118–19
anxiety, 66
Aquinnah, Massachusetts, 143
arguments, in legislative research report, 70–71
arts, engaging with public through, 134–35
assignments: advocacy portfolio, 155; advocacy video, 145; bill choice, 38; bringing the world to your classroom, 135–36; capitol tour, 105–8, 118–20; community celebration event, 151–53, 160–61; contacting potential collaborators, 53, 55–57; for culminating experience, 150–55; current events/issues review, 24; elevator speech, 112–13, 122; final legislative report, 154; final presentation, 153–54, 160–61; function of, 117; group check-ins, 103–5; guidelines for ENACT course, 36–38; individual and group check-ins, 101, 103–5; issue brief, 38–39; for legislative research, 69–74; legislative research report, 69–72, 76–78; lessons-learned presentation, 154, 161–62; meeting/reflection journal, 113–14, 125; meeting-script, 111–12; one-pager, 72–74, 80–83, 84, 85–91; op-ed, 131, 144–45; panel discussion, 102, 108–11, 120–21; pitch, 112–13; planning, 38; policy brief, 72, 129, 130, 136–44; prenup, 36–37; present and

defend activity, 148, 150–51, 159–60; public, 129–34; public testimony, 113, 122–24; reflection, 155; sample guidelines for, 36–38; sharing with community groups, 133–34; social media, 131–33, 145; stakeholder analysis worksheet, 78–80; syllabus, 22–23
Austin, Texas, 143

belonging, 95–96
Bhojwani, Sayu, 115
bill: addressing fate of, 149; arguments against, 70–71; becoming an expert of, 60; choosing, 62–66; consequences of passing, 66; constitutionality of, 71; controversy regarding, 64–65; external–interest regarding, 64–65; external–perception regarding, 65; factors in choosing, 63; failure of, 65, 68–69, 149; familiarity with, 67; feasibility regarding, 65; fiscal impact of, 71; hero of, 79; identity in, 64; as inactive, 68–69; internal–interest regarding, 64; internal–perception regarding, 64; to oppose, 68; outside work on, by public, 127–28; overview and background of, 70; passion for, 64; pivots regarding, 68–69; searching for, 60; students as experts of, 102; to support, 68; types of, for choosing, 62–66; victim of, 79; villain of, 79
bill choice assignment, 38
bloggers, 61
Boston, Massachusetts, 143
Brandeis, Louis, 41
brief, issue, 38–39

California, 17, 41, 48, 87, 142, 143
campaign cycle, 50
campus career center, 156
campus volunteer/service programs, 158
Cantor, Alison, 129
capacity, 104
capitol tour, 105–8, 118–20
Carroll, Morgan, 53–54
check–ins, 101, 103–5
chemicals, 141
civic advocacy groups, 44
civic crisis, in education, 2–3
Clark, Lieutenant, 91
class culture, 95, 115–16
Class Distinctions and Income Brackets (Resource Generation), 115–16
class logistics, considerations regarding, 16–17
class mobility, 116
class readings, 114–16
class sessions, at state legislature, 96–97
collaboration, 5–6, 20–21, 53
colonialism, 118
committee/commission meetings and hearings, as resource, 75–76
community: celebration event, 151–53, 160–61; cultivation of, with students, 100–102; ENACT as model for advocacy training in, 8; groups, sharing with, 133–34; partners, 156–57
Congress, term limits of, 59
Connecticut, 87, 88, 138, 143–44
Connecticut General Assembly, 20
constitutionality, of the bill, 71
content learning objective, 167
controversy, in bill choice, 64–65
course structure, in syllabus, 23. *See also* ENACT course
Covid-19 pandemic, 98
culminating experience: additional resources for, 155–58; addressing fate of bill in, 149; advising resources for, 156; advocacy portfolio for, 155; assessing learning outcomes in,

149–50; assignments for, 150–55; campus career center for, 156; campus volunteer/service programs for, 158; celebration in, 159; community celebration event for, 151–53, 160–61; community partners for, 156–57; considerations regarding, 148; context of end of class in, 148–49; department internship programs for, 157–58; final legislative report assignment for, 154; final presentation assignment for, 153–54, 160–61; importance of, 147; key course components for, 150–55; lessons-learned presentation for, 154, 161–62; overview of, 158–59; present and defend activity for, 150–51, 159–60; reflection assignments for, 155; social/alumni networks for, 157
Cultivation of the Northwest (murals), 118
current events/issues review, 24
Cuyahoga, Ohio, 143
cynicism, 169

Dakota people, 118–19
Democratic control, 61
department internship programs, 157–58
Derek Bok Center for Teaching and Learning (Harvard University), 24
descriptive representation, 96
disciplinary context, of ENACT course, 148–49
Discoverers and Civilizers Led to the Source of the Mississippi (mural), 119
dress code, at state legislature, 99–100
drought, 89

education, civic crisis in, 2–3
Elazar, Daniel, 60
elevator pitch models, 116–17
elevator speech assignment, 112–13, 122
email: to advocacy groups, 136; ignoring, 50–51, 109–10; introductory, 53; sample script for, 55–56, 136; thank you, 111
emergency responders, 91
ENACT course: adaptability of, 8; assignment guidelines for, 36–38; celebration following, 159; challenges in, 93; class logistics for, 16–17; collaboration in, 20–21; community cultivation in, 100–102; constraints regarding, 117; content learning objective of, 167; course calendar structure for, 19–20; course descriptions for, 26–28; course model of, 5–6, 10; cynicism regarding, 169; defined, 2; disciplinary context of, 148–49; enacting, 168–70; as evidence-based, 7, 163–66; expansion of, 4; experiential learning in, 6–7; financial resources for, 97–98; flexibility of, 15, 16; as fun, 8; goal of, 68, 168; institutional features for, 16–17; as interdisciplinary, 8; justice in, 4; key questions regarding, 16–22; knowledge in, 4; learning objectives for, 28–29; life after, 11–12; mission of, 4; as modular, 7–8; opportunities in, 93–94; overview of, 4–5; personal testimony from, 5, 6, 13, 19, 20, 49, 53, 67, 72, 100, 108, 117, 129, 131, 148, 159, 166, 170; platform for, 25; political environment for, 17–19; purpose of, 6–8; report regarding, 164–66; resources for, 17, 24–26; sample schedules for, 29–35; skills in, 4; skills learning objective of, 167; student belonging in, 95–96; student makeup for, 16; survey results regarding, 164–66; syllabus for, 22–23; timing for, 17; travel considerations in, 97–98; values learning objective of, 167
Engines of Democracy (Rosenthal), 114–15

Entangled and Ingested project, 134–35
EPIC laser talk model, 116–17
executive summary, 72
expansion narrative, 118
exploration, 119

Facebook, 132, 145
factsheet, in legislative research, 72, 73
faculty/instructors: active learning model for, 15; adaptability and responsiveness modeling by, 102–3, 110; capacity of, 104; capitol tour by, 105–8, 118–20; care and concern by, 101–2; check-ins by, 101, 103–5; class logistics considerations of, 16–17; collaboration considerations of, 20–21; course calendar structure considerations of, 19–20; cynicism to, 169; in ENACT course model, 5–6; hesitancy considerations of, 21–22; political environment considerations of, 17–19; preparation of, 104; as resources, 26; resources considerations of, 17; student makeup considerations of, 16; traditional methods of, 15
Father Hennepin Discovering the Falls of St. Anthony (painting), 119
feasibility, in bill choice, 65
federal funding, 138–39
fictionalized story, for in-class use, 81–82
final legislative report assignment, 154
final presentation assignment, 153–54, 160–61
fiscal impact, of the bill, 71
follow-up, following public testimony, 124
From Shore to Statehouse grant, 138

Gardner, Marian, 100
Gender, Race/Ethnicity, and Representation in State Legislatures (Reingold), 115
good governance advocacy, 65
group check-ins, 101, 103–5
group meeting log, 125
guest speakers, 135–36

hard ask, 112
HB 637, 91
healthcare, 28
Hennepin, Louis, 119
higher education, battles in, 62
honesty, in advocacy, 67
Honolulu, Hawaii, 143
hook, 113, 122

identity, in bill choice, 64
Indigenous people, 118–19
individual check-ins, 101, 103–5
infrastructure bills, 61
Instagram, 132, 145
institutions/universities: culture of fear in, 62; damage control by, 22; features and class setting of, 16–17; hesitancy of, 21–22; as living laboratory, 74; as political actors, 49; student belonging in, 95–96; support from, 49
instructors. *See* faculty/instructors
internship, 19–20, 157–58
interviews, in one-pager, 81
invasive species, 141
issue brief, 38–39

Jensen, Barbara, 116
journal, meeting/reflection, 113–14, 125
justice focus, in ENACT course, 4

knowledge focus, in ENACT course, 4

laser talk model, 116–17
learning objectives, 23, 28–29
learning outcomes, assessing, 149–50
leave-behind, in legislative research, 72, 73

legislative assistants (LAs), 108, 109–10, 111
legislative calendar guide (NSCL), 54
legislative database, 75
legislative library, 75
legislative research: advocacy organizations for, 75; amount as necessary of, 66–67; assignments for, 69–74; caution regarding, 73–74; committee and commission meetings and hearings for, 75–76; key course components for, 69–74; legislative database for, 75; legislative library for, 75; one-pager in, 72–74, 80–83, 84, 85–91; overview of, 10–11, 59–60; report for, 69–72, 76–78; research resources for, 76; resources for, 67, 75–76; safeguards regarding, 73–74; skills and norms of, 67; stakeholder analysis worksheet for, 78–80
lessons-learned presentation, 154, 161–62
Lin, Maya, 134
lobbying, defined, 47
lobbyists, 46–47, 59, 94–95
local legislature, advocacy visits with, 18
local news sources, 24–25, 61, 94
logistics, for relationship building, 50–52

Maine, 42, 90
Malibu, California, 143
Massachusetts, 17, 89
meeting/reflection journal, 113–14, 125
meeting-script assignment, 111–12
Miller, Gail, 12
Minnesota, 75, 95, 118–20
Mississippi, 60
Mississippi River, 119
modularity, of ENACT model, 7–8
Montana, 17

National Conference of State Legislatures (NCSL), 54
National Oceanic and Atmospheric Administration (NOAA), 138
Nebraska, 41
Nevada, 25
New Hampshire, 41, 48
New Jersey, 143
New Mexico, 41
news deserts, 25, 61, 131
New York, 48, 143
Nicholas Institute's Plastics Policy Inventory, 143
nonpartisan staff, in state legislature, 46
North Dakota, 17

one-pager, 72–74, 80–83, 84, 85–91
op-ed, 131, 144–45
orientation visit, at state capitol, 97

Pacific Rim, 142
panel discussion, 102, 108–11, 120–21
partisan control of the state, 61
partisan staff, in state legislature, 45–46
passion, in bill choice, 64
PBLWorks (Buck Institute for Education), 24
People Like Us (Bhojwani), 115
Pevide, Elaina, 49
pitch assignment, 112–13
planning, 38, 50–52
plastic pollution, 87, 88, 134–35, 138, 139–44
policy advocacy, 1, 2, 4–5, 22, 46–47. *See also* advocates/citizen advocates; specific aspects
policy brief, 72, 129, 130, 136–44
policy summary, 74
political context, in legislative research report, 71
political culture, variations of, 60
political decision-making, state level of, 7
political environment, institutional features of, 17–19

political journalists, 47–48
political science education, 166–68
Politics in Action course, 1–2
pollution, plastic, 87, 88, 134–35, 138, 139–44
position statement, 81
power mapping, 43–44
pre-advocacy class sessions, at state capitol, 96–97
prenup agreement, 36–37
prescription costs, 90
present and defend activity, 148, 150–51, 159–60
presentation assignment, final, 153–54
The Progress of the State (statue), 118
public: additional resources regarding, 134–36; arts engagement with, 134–35; assignments regarding, 129–34; best results with, 129; communication with, 129; engaging with, 11, 127; key components regarding, 129–34; key questions in engaging with, 127–29; outreach to, 129; sharing with community groups in, 133–34; winning support from, 127
public-facing aspect, of legislative research report, 71
public testimony assignment, 113, 122–24

question and answer, with legislators, 110–11

Reading Classes (Jensen), 116
readings/assignments, in syllabus, 23
recommendations section, in legislative research report, 72
recruitment, for panel discussion, 108–9
recycling, 134–35
reflection, 113–14, 125, 147, 161
reflection assignments, 155
Reingold, Beth, 115
relationship building, at state legislature: assignments in, 53; beginning process of, 43–44; clarity in, 51; contact process in, 53; gratitude in, 52; institutional support for, 49; key questions regarding, 43–52; obstacles to, 50–51; overview of, 41–43; payoff in, 52; persistence in, 51; planning and logistics for, 50–52; sample email script for potential collaborator in, 55–56; sample phone/Zoom script for potential collaborator in, 56–57; sustaining, 50; useful individuals for, 44–48
report, legislative research, 69–72, 76–78
reproductive rights legislation, 61
Republican control, 61
resentment, of students, 105
Resource Generation, 115–16
resources: advising, 156; for building relationships, 53–54; campus career center, 156; campus volunteer/service programs, 158; class readings as, 114–16; community partners, 156–57; considerations regarding, 17; for culminating experience, 155–58; department internship programs, 157–58; elevator pitch models, 116–17; for engaging with the public, 134–36; for legislative research, 75–76; for life after ENACT, 155–58; for meeting with legislatures, 114–17; social/alumni networks, 157; for teaching ENACT course, 24–26
responsiveness, 102–3, 110
RESULTS, 117
Rhode Island, 75
risks, in syllabus, 23
Roanoke, Virginia, 143
Rosenthal, Alan, 114–15
Rosenthal, Sage, 19

scaffolding, 98–99, 133
schedule, ENACT course, 29–35
skills focus, in ENACT course, 4
skills learning objective, 167
social/alumni networks, as resource, 49, 61, 157, 165–66
social media, 131–33, 145
stakeholder analysis worksheet, 78–80
stakeholders, in legislative research report, 71
St. Anthony Falls, Minnesota, 119
state legislature: accessibility of, 17–18; adaptability regarding, 102–3; advocates to, 59; anxiety regarding, 66, 93; campaign cycle of, 50; capitol tour of, 105–8, 118–20; characteristics of, 94–95; citizen–legislator model of, 17–18; class sessions at, 96–97; cultural and political contexts of, 60–62; demographics of, 18–19, 43–44, 94–95, 115; descriptive representation and, 96; dress code at, 99–100; economic class of, 95; employment in, 156; environment as foreign to students, 93; follow-up with, 124; formality in, 99; full time, 17; hesitancy regarding, 21–22; higher education battles in, 62; ideological and partisan makeup of, 60–61; internships in, 157–58; as intimidating, 99; as laboratories of democracy, 41; lobbyists in, 46–47, 59, 94–95; locations of, 97–98, 148; meeting with, 11; nonpartisan staff in, 46; openness and accountability of, 61–62; orientation visit with, 97; panel discussion with, 102, 108–11, 120–21; partisan staff in, 45–46; planning visits to, 98–99; policy advocates in, 46–47; policymaking capacity in, 8; political culture of, 60; political decision-making in, 7; political environment of, 17–19; political journalists in, 47–48; politics of, 18–19; professionalization in, 156; question and answer time with, 110–11; rhythm of session of, 50; rules and norms of, 98, 99–100; staff demographics and characteristics in, 94–95; structure variations of, 45; student belonging in, 95–96; term limits for, 45; variations of, 50; virtual visits to, 18, 98; websites of, 25. *See also* legislative research; relationship building, at state legislature
state news sources, 24–25
storybook/storycard, 72, 73, 74, 81, 86–91, 129
storytelling, through the arts, 134–35
students: activity tracking by, 113–14; adaptability of, 102–3, 110; anxiety of, 66; belonging and, 95–96; capacity of, 104; care and concern for, 101–2; check-ins of, 101, 103–5; classism of, 115–16; collaboration among, 101; community cultivation with, 100–102; demographic characteristics of, 95–96; descriptive representation and, 96; as digital native, 133; diversity of, 148; expert role of, 102; familiarity by, 67; lessons for, 69; makeup of, 16; pivoting by, 68–69; planning of legislative visits by, 98–99; practicing by, 66–67; public speaking by, 101; as reaching out to advocacy organizations, 128; resentment by, 105; responsiveness of, 102–3, 110; rights and privileges of, 99; risk taking by, 101–2; rules and norms for, 98, 99–100; scaffolding with, 133; survey of, 164. *See also* advocates/citizen advocates

stylized posters, 134
subnational government, defined, 27
syllabus, 22–23

Take Back Your Government (Carroll), 53–54
Teams, 135
term limits, 45, 59
testimony, public, 113
thank you cards, 111
TikTok, 132–33, 145
tour, capitol, 105–8, 118–20

unions, 44
United Kingdom, 142–43
universities. *See* institutions/universities
University of Hartford, 20

values learning objective, 167
Vermont, 48
video, advocacy, 145
Vietnam War Memorial, 134
Virginia, 25, 83n5, 91
virtual visits, 18, 98
volunteer organizations, governmental relations specialists in, 44
volunteer/service programs, 158
Voting Rights Act, 115

Washington (DC), 46
Washington (state), 83n4
Weigel, Taylor, 67
word-for-word script assignment, 111–12
working-class people, 115, 116
"Working with Legislators" handbook (NSCL), 54
Works Project Administration, 134

X (Twitter), 132

YouTube, 145

Zoom, 135

Brandeis Series in Law and Society

Rosalind Kabrhel, J.D. and Daniel Breen, J.D., Editors

Justice Louis D. Brandeis once said that "if we desire respect for the law, we must first make the law respectable." For Justice Brandeis, making the law "respectable" meant making it work in the interests of humankind, as a help rather than a hindrance in the manifold struggles of persons of all backgrounds to achieve justice. In that spirit, the Law and Society Series publishes works that take interdisciplinary approaches to law, drawing richly from the social sciences and humanities, with a view towards shedding critical light upon the variety of ways in which legal rules, and the institutions that enforce them, affect our lives. Intended for practitioners, academics, students, and the interested general public, this series will feature titles that contribute robustly to contemporary debates about law and legal reform, all with a view towards adding to efforts of all sorts to make the law "respectable."

For a complete list of books that are available in the series, visit https://brandeisuniversitypress.com/series/law

ENACTing Change: A Handbook for Teaching Advocacy and Civic Engagement
Kathleen Cole, Rob Glover, Michelle Inderbitzin, Richard Meagher, and Katharine Owens, edited by Melissa Stimell

Unlocking Learning: International Perspectives on Education in Prison
Justin McDevitt and Mneesha Gellman

We're Here to Help: When Guardianship Goes Wrong
Diane Dimond

The Common Flaw: Needless Complexity in the Courts and 50 Ways to Reduce It
Thomas Moukawsher

Education Behind the Wall: Why and How We Teach College in Prison
Mneesha Gellman

